SUMMIT
DEVOTIONAL

A 12-week workbook to help men renew their faith, strengthen relationships and solidify sexual integrity

BY: **JASON B. MARTINKUS, M.A.**

Copyright © 2017 by Jason B. Martinkus, M.A.

This title is available at www.redmeptiveliving.com.

Published by Redemptive Living Publishing
	Denver, CO 80210

ISBN: 978-0-692-96220-6

All rights reserved. No part of this publication may be reproduced, stored in a retrieval system, or transmitted in any form by any means, electronic, mechanical, photocopy, recording or otherwise, without the prior permission of the publisher, except as provided by USA copyright law.

Unless otherwise indicated, Scripture quotations are taken from the Holy Bible, New International Version (NIV)®. Copyright © 1973, 1978, 1984 by International Bible Society. Used by permission of Zondervan Publishing House. All rights reserved.

Scripture quotations marked *MSG* are taken from The Message by Eugene H. Peterson, Copyright © 1993, 1994, 1995, 2000, 2001, 2002. Used by permission of Navpress Publishing Group. All rights reserved.

Feelings Chart on page 18 is used by permission from http://blogs.oregonstate.edu/careerservices/2012/11/30/emotional-intelligence-what-is-it-and-why-do-employers-want-emotionally-intelligent-employees/.

Feelings Wheel on page 17 is used by permission from Dr. Gloria Willcox, Westminster Shores, Villa 20, 125 57th Ave South, St. Petersburg, FL 33705.

Printed in the United States of America.
Cover and interior design by CreativePickle and Hudson Design Works.
Cover Photo: © iStockphoto. Used with permission.
Printed in the United States of America.

TABLE OF CONTENTS

INTRO 1

HOW TO USE THIS DEVOTIONAL WORKBOOK 3

MISSION 5

NOT CONDEMNED 10

SWEET EMOTIONS 13

(IN)SIGNIFICANCE 19

MIND GAMES 22

REWIRED 26

SELF-AWARE 30

HANDPICKED 34

LONGING 37

TO WHOM 40

CLEAN CLOTHES 44

INSTINCT 49

PROTECTION 54

OBEDIENCE 57

DAILY MANNA 60

SHAME DETOX 64

SELF-DEFEAT 68

THE DEVIL MADE ME DO IT 71

REMINDERS 76

RIPCORD 79

SELF-CONTROL 82

COMFORT 85

IDOL TIME	88
TRAVEL LIGHTER	91
STOP STEALING	94
PATIENCE	99
AFFLICTION	102
DIVINE DISRUPTIONS	105
TRUTH TELLING	109
GOOD MORNING	112
(RE)COMMITMENT	117
HIGH VISIBILITY	120
JUST VISITING	123
GIVING	126
HAS MAT	129
LEGACY	133
CLOSING	138
ABOUT THE AUTHOR	139

INTRO

Early in my journey of recovery from sexual integrity issues, well-meaning Christian folk would tell me I needed to read the Bible if I really wanted to change. Being a Christian, I knew that was true, and I knew it was in fact the "right" thing to be doing. But there were two problems: first, I didn't know where to start. So I would play Bible Roulette and simply thumb across the edge of the book, randomly stop and crack it open. Inevitably, it seems like I landed on pages detailing the death, eternal damnation, and judgment of people in sexual sin. That led to the second problem: I didn't know enough about the Bible to translate what I was reading into anything helpful, encouraging or motivational. It just seemed to perpetuate the shame and self-hatred I already felt. Beyond that, it further exacerbated my idea of God as a cosmic killjoy who looks down on His people with scrutiny, waiting to catch us doing something wrong. Blah!

Somewhere along the way, with the help of friends, church, and, later, seminary, I began to read the Scripture differently. What started to pop out were verses that shined light on God's mercy and grace, things that made sense for living in real time, today. I started to find guidance and actual, applicable, practical tools to do life better. Instead of reading through a lens of shame and condemnation, I was reading as a son receiving guidance from his dad. I started to feel understood, significant, and encouraged. God actually knew what He was talking about!

Today, I still struggle with betting on black but landing on red when I play Bible Roulette. Sometimes I lose the bet and feel frustrated and wonder if God is listening. There are droughts and that feeling of just "checking the box"—reading the Bible just to say I did, but without really getting anything out of it. But more often, it seems like something comes to light that fits the current state of my life. The truths can be hard-hitting, like a punch in the gut. But that's the nature of the beast; the Word cuts deep, dividing joint and marrow (Hebrews 4:12). And yet, it is also incredibly informative and helpful, giving voice to God's guidance (2 Timothy 3:15-17). There is also comfort and encouragement, especially the more I can visualize the Biblical characters in present-day circumstances. In the journey towards sexual integrity and wholeness, many of these truths have stuck with me and helped me maintain my walk. This devotional is my attempt to share some of them with you.

My hope is that as you engage the material you'll find some new angles that illuminate things you've not seen before. I want it to be profoundly practical. Yes, I expect that some of these things will tap into your shame. It did mine just writing it! And yes, I do expect some things won't make sense. There are some things that we'll only ever understand by the Holy Spirit interacting with our spirit, and that will happen in God's timing.

I also expect that some of the devotionals will be encouraging and inspiring; that you'll meditate on them seeing God in His infinite mercy and sufficient grace. And right in the middle of all that I hope you'll find yourself choosing integrity, honor, and dignity over sexual acting out. You can do it!

HOW TO USE THIS DEVOTIONAL WORKBOOK

When I designed these devos they weren't meant to simply be read and reflected on. I had in mind that they would be exercises in intimacy—being known and knowing. On the journey towards wholeness and sanctification, we must be connected with our own hearts, the hearts of other people, and to the heart of God. As we move into deeper intimacy with each of these, we'll find ourselves farther from acting out sexually again.

Each devo has a Self, God, and Others section. The Self questions are meant to stir your heart and mind. I hope some of them squeeze emotion out of you. If that happens, it means the content is tapping into something that needs attention. Spend some time there; don't just cruise past that.

The God section includes suggestions and guidance on how to pray as it pertains to that particular devotional. Sometimes those prayers are invitations to God, sometimes requests, and often simply gratitude. The goal of this section is to lead you to pray specifically about what lies at the root of the problem, rather than the symptoms themselves. If the "problem"—the symptoms—goes away but the root isn't dealt with, are we any better off? I'd say not really. We don't want a behavior change without a heart change beneath it. After each God section, take time to write your prayer.

Then there is the Others section. I encourage you to talk to at least one other person and invite them to walk through this with you. Ideally it would be someone with whom you can dialogue honestly about what you are experiencing. If you are single, that would be a trusted friend, mentor, or accountability partner. If you are married that might be your wife, but it also needs to be someone outside of her. Again, a friend, mentor, pastor, or accountability partner are great options. I want those relationships to grow, strengthen, and deepen as a result of your work in this book. Don't buy the lie that it would be a pain, inconvenience, or bending-over-backwards for someone else to engage this with you. That's what friends and fellow travelers on the journey are for! After each Others section, there is space to make notes of key points or meaningful feedback you receive.

Finally, some of the chapters have Take Action sections, with a specific action step to follow through on. The idea is to move us farther along personally, spiritually, and relationally by living out some of what we're learning.

Functionally, the material is divided into twelve weeks, each with three devotionals. You're obviously welcome to take them at your own speed, but the idea is to have a rhythm of two during the week and one on the weekend. Some you may need a couple extra days to chew on, some will go faster. I do encourage you to pace yourself; don't just breeze through them. Give this a chance to be an investment that pays a real dividend.

All that said, it's time to get moving!

MISSION

> **Luke 4:18-19**
>
> *The Spirit of the Lord is on me,*
> *because he has anointed me*
> *to proclaim good news to the poor.*
> *He has sent me to proclaim freedom for the prisoners*
> *and recovery of sight for the blind,*
> *to set the oppressed free,*
> *to proclaim the year of the Lord's favor.*

DEVO

Begin with the end in mind.

The verse for this devo can be thought of as Jesus' personal mission statement. It outlined the reason He was here. It informed His modus operandi and defined His day-to-day life. Should anyone question His intent, they need only to look at this personal mission statement. Each line depicts the passionate, pointed direction He was moving.

His mission is tangible—he literally set prisoners free and caused blind people to see. His mission is also allegorical—he came to offer a larger freedom; from death. He came to offer a different kind of sight; eyes to see the living God. He sets prisoners free, not just from jail but from the enslaving sin of self. Finally, he came to proclaim the year of the Lord's favor—the year of Jubilee. It is important to understand that the year of Jubilee was a time of universal pardon. All sins were forgiven, slaves were set free, debts were erased and canceled. In other words, all burdens to a heavy heart and all hindrances to a full life were removed. Everybody got a sort of mulligan for the soul.

That's why Jesus walked the planet.

Why do you?

You may be thinking, "What does this have to do with sexual integrity?" The answer is: everything. If we don't have a mission we want to wake up for, we'll try to escape what we have to wake up for.

Be thinking about your own personal mission statement. The next section, Self, will help with that. At the end of the MISSION lesson you'll have a chance to write your own statement.

Press on!

 **SELF**

Why do you believe you are on the planet?

How has your sexual sin kept you from fulfilling what you believe to be God's call on your life?

🙏 GOD

Ask God to inform your mission statement and pray that He'll be glorified by how you live it out. Invite Him to show you in Scripture what your mission might include. Write this prayer out below.

OTHERS

While you're thinking about your personal mission statement, talk with your connections about it. What do they think is a meaningful mission? Have they created their own statements—and if so, what are they?

Below are a few sample mission statements that others have developed while doing this devo. Maybe it will spark you to develop, add to, or tweak yours.

"I'm on a mission to surrender my thoughts, my feelings, my actions, my decisions, and my responsibilities to Jesus. I'll live out this surrender through daily prayer, devotional work like reading and writing, and fellowship. This surrender will transform me into the husband, father, and man that God created me to be."

"In the next 12 weeks I want to live out each day drawing closer to God; begin to

heal by letting the power of God work in my life; recognize that I am powerless and in need of God to heal me; and create daily habits that are God centered."

"I will fight the good fight and not lose hope when things get hard. I will turn to my knees when in the past I would escape or give up; Lord, protect me from the fiery darts of the enemy. I will make choices with the end in mind. I want to re-write history for my self and my family."

TAKE ACTION

In one or two sentences, write a personal mission statement that describes what you are committed to and aiming for over the course of this devotional.

After you've written this statement and feel good about it, I want you to be reminded of it. So, right now, turn to the following pages 9, 43, 75, 108, and 132 and jot it down there as well. That way you'll have some reminders of why you are fighting the good fight. You never know, you may happen to land on it exactly when you need it the most.

Also, I'd love to know what your personal mission statement is! You can jump on the website, **www.summitdevo.com**, and enter it there when you get a chance. You'll also find some additional resources for the journey there.

MY PERSONAL MISSION STATEMENT

NOT CONDEMNED

> **Romans 8:1**
>
> *Therefore, there is now no condemnation for those who are in Christ Jesus.*

DEVO

One of the things I love most about this verse is that it functions as a huge sigh of relief on the heels of the verses preceding it. Romans 7:7-25 gives voice to what so many of us experience in our struggle for sexual purity. Here is Paul, a hero of the faith, wrestling with that part of himself that he can't seem to corral. Some twelve-step programs call it "my addict," some call it the "shadow" or "the imposter," and some refer to the Biblical notion of the "old self/man." It's that part of ourselves that we despise. We want so badly to do the right thing and stop the bad things, but it seems no matter how fervently we swear it's the last time, inevitably it isn't. We take steps we think will fix the problem, but we only trim the tree branches rather than extract the roots. I once frisbee'd a laptop into a dumpster thinking I wouldn't act out again if I just denied myself access. Within days I had a new laptop and I went back to my sexual sin again. Sound familiar?

Here's the good news: no matter how many times you do what you don't want to do, Romans 8:1 is there; you are not condemned. God has not turned His back on you. He receives you with open arms.

SELF

Can you relate to the idea of swearing every time is the last time? Have you ever bargained with God with regards to sin ("If you'll take this away then I'll be a missionary in Zimbabwe!")?

Have you believed the lie, like I did, that getting rid of internet access is the answer to your struggle? (ex: Throw away a laptop, believe filters will stop you, get a dumb-phone).

What steps have you taken to deal with sexual sin that ultimately proved to only be "trimming the branches" rather than getting to the root?

Have you been on the precipice of believing God has given up on you? When and why?

GOD

Invite God to show you the roots of your struggle. Pray for Him to make the idea of freedom from condemnation real. Give thanks for grace, for the sacrifice of Jesus, and for the patience of God.

 OTHERS

Ask the guys in your group—or your wife, or whomever you've chosen as your accountability partner—to remind you regularly that you are not condemned. Tell them about the time(s) when you've felt like God might be giving up on you. Ask for accountability to fight the lies of condemnation that pop into your head.

TAKE ACTION

Read Romans 7.

Recite Romans 8:1 aloud three times, personalizing the language. (e.g. "Therefore I, (*your name here*), am not condemned, because I, (*your name here*) am in Christ Jesus.")

I urge you to do this every day from now until you're done with this book.

SWEET EMOTIONS

> **Psalm 135:14**
>
> *For the LORD will vindicate his people*
> *   and have **compassion** on his servants.*
>
> **Jeremiah 31:3**
>
> *The LORD appeared to us in the past, saying:*
> *"I have **loved** you with an everlasting love;*
> *I have drawn you with unfailing **kindness**."*
>
> **Luke 10:21**
>
> *At that time Jesus, full of **joy** through the Holy Spirit...*
>
> **John 11:35**
>
> *Jesus **wept**.*
>
> **Deuteronomy 9:22b (MSG)**
>
> *...more occasions when you made GOD **furious** with you.*

DEVO

Sweet emotions. No I'm not talking about the education we got from the great theologians Aerosmith. I'm talking about *Imago Dei*; the theological concept that we are created in the image of God. And our God is a feeling God.

As you read the Old Testament you quickly see that He is an emotional being. He is angry, compassionate, loving, and kind to name a few. And we're created in His image. He yearns for relationship with His people, grieves over our sinful behavior, and rejoices in our repentance and return to Himself.

The New Testament depicts the God-man, Jesus, as a feeler as well. We see Him exhibiting love, connection, grief, sorrow, and joy. If you're like me, you may believe that you don't know how to engage emotionally, lack an emotional vocabulary, and sometimes even view the emotional aspect of yourself as faulty or errant. Emotions have gotten a bad rap. People say you can't trust them, shouldn't make decisions based on them, and the way of following your heart is for the irresponsible. There is truth in all these statements, however, the implicit assumption and unintended consequence is to believe emotions are bad or wrong.

Emotions are real, valid and legitimate; and simultaneously often a poor basis for decision making. They are intricately woven into our humanity. To ignore or deny them is to deny a part of our created design.

The struggle with sexual sin is an emotional issue. When we try not to feel, we actually end up suppressing our emotions and ultimately they come out in other ways. Many of us have sexualized our emotions and use our sexuality as the vehicle to feel.

People will often say the lure is the excitement, the sense of adventure, the passion. In other words, when they act out sexually, they can actually feel. But it is a fraudulent way of tapping into those emotions. We have to allow ourselves to feel, to experience joy and pain, suffering and solace, comfort and conviction. Further (and this is difficult to even write) some of us have to give ourselves permission to cry. Yes, grown men can shed tears. Jesus Himself modeled this for us. In fact, if you do a little research, you'll find that as humans we have a unique emotional tear that isn't present in other mammals. This emotional tear releases toxins *from* the body as well as endorphins *within* the body. In other words, crying biochemically makes us feel better.

When we act out sexually we're manufacturing an emotional response within ourselves. We look for imagery and seek out people who make us feel loved, connected, wanted, excited, adventurous, powerful, and adequate. Endorphins are released. We'll talk more on this in another devo. But for now, know that sex is emotional. Deep down, our hearts are longing to feel something that sex and orgasm can't supply. We long to express emotions but many of us have closed the valve somewhere in life so the waterworks are turned off.

It is an important part of recovery to be attuned to what is happening in our hearts and to allow ourselves to feel. It's how Jesus lived.

👤 SELF

What's your take on emotions? Are they good? Bad? Valid? Some men view emotions as a feminine attribute; do you?

Have you given yourself permission to experience heartbreak to the point of tears? Or joy to the point of tears? When was the last time you actually let yourself cry?

 ## GOD

Do you view God as an emotional, relational, loving Father God? Or as the emotionless, stoic, possibly disengaged creator God? Ask Him to reveal His true nature and character to you. Also, ask Him to show you your true, deepest emotions. Ask Him to help you experience heartbreak for the things His heart breaks for and excitement for what he gets excited about. Ask Him to help you feel love for those He loves.

 **OTHERS**

If you are married, talk with your wife about your ability and/or willingness to connect with your emotions. Invite her feedback.

Whether married or single, do the same with your connections. Ask them if they consider you connected or disconnected emotionally. Have they ever seen you cry? Have you seen them cry?

Also, talk about what makes you feel excited. More specifically, what things that matter in life make you excited? It's easy to feel excited when our favorite sports team wins, but we're trying to go deeper than that here.

 TAKE ACTION

Right now, take a minute to assess your emotions. What do you feel? Happy? Sad? Annoyed at the exercise?

Each day this week spend ten total minutes considering your emotions. You can do five minutes in the morning and five at night, or you can check in several times throughout the day. Remember, good, fine, and tired don't count (nor any variation thereof: okay, better, great, bad, terrible, etc.). Go deeper and really assess what you're feeling and why.

Here are a couple of tools to help with identifying emotions. Use them when you check in with yourself and are trying to put words to what you're feeling.

FEELINGS WHEEL DIAGRAM

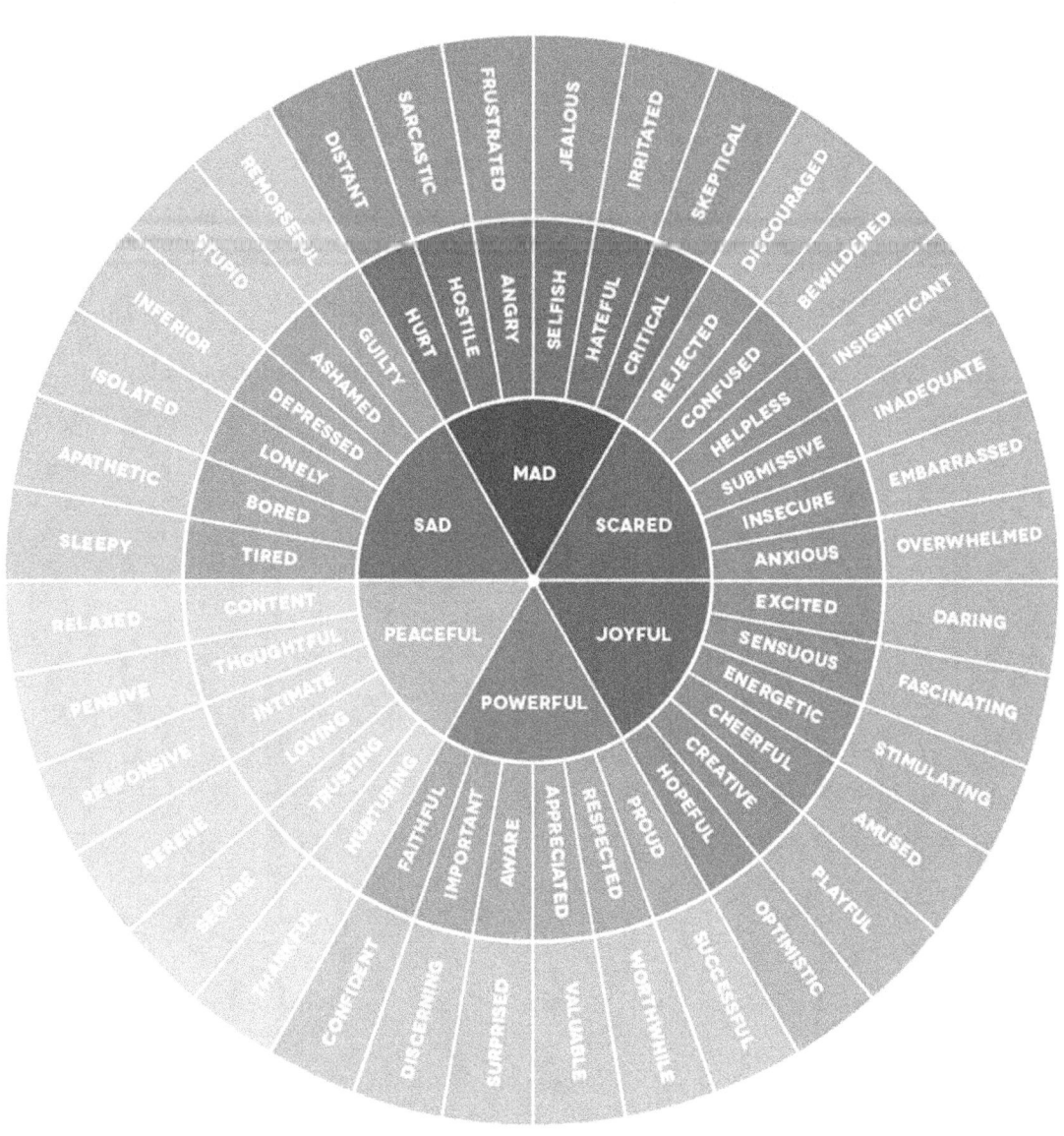

SWEET EMOTIONS

(IN)SIGNIFICANCE

> **Luke 4:9-13**
>
> *The devil led him to Jerusalem and had him stand on the highest point of the temple. "If you are the Son of God," he said, "throw yourself down from here. For it is written: 'He will command his angels concerning you to guard you carefully; they will lift you up in their hands, so that you will not strike your foot against a stone.'"*

DEVO

Satan loves to twist scripture. That was his tactic with Adam and Eve, with Jesus, and it is with us too. When we look closely, we can see Satan twisting the words not just to be confusing, not just to cause us to doubt God, but also to tap a deeper nerve. He knows how to get at our hearts and how to prick some of the innermost insecurities we have. Ultimately, he questions God, asserting that God is not who he says is and will not follow through on his promises. In this temptation we see Satan tapping the nerve of insignificance in two ways.

First, he questions Jesus' sonship. "IF you are the son of God." See how subtle that is? Satan is calling into question whether Jesus even resides in the royal family! Satan would love for Jesus to question His true identity. And he would love it if we questioned our true identity as children of the most high God as well.

The second way Satan indicts Jesus' significance flows from the first. He suggests that Jesus test God to prove His worth and value; to see if the Father actually loves him. If Jesus, the son, really matters to His father, then He won't let the son hurt Himself, right? It's as if Satan was sarcastically saying, "If you really are the Son of God, whom God so dearly loves, then prove it! Make God prove He cares about you." Satan is not only questioning Jesus' sonship but also God's love for His children.

Perhaps you've felt this in your own life. Maybe there have been moments when you questioned whether you really matter to God. "If He really loves me, why wouldn't he deliver me from sexual sin?" you may ask. Satan's desire is for you is to question your sonship and God's love for you. Don't buy the lie! He already proved His infinite love by sending His son to die for you. You are a child of the King!

Remember, Satan would love for you feel insignificant. Don't forget that you matter, and people need you.

 SELF

What lies have you been believing regarding how God feels about you? What messages has Satan used to try and convince you that you don't matter to God?

Do you find yourself wishing God would prove His love for you? If so, what would that look like? How could that happen in a way that you would actually believe it?

🙏 GOD

Thank God for your sonship and your inclusion in the Royal family. Thank Him for Living Proof of His love. Invite Him to give you a clear picture of how He really feels about you.

👥 OTHERS

Discuss what it means to be a child of the King. If you lived out of that identity, how would it change your life?

Share any of the lies you identified in your self-reflection. Ask your accountability partners what lies they believe, and pay attention to what you feel and think when you hear them. How can you be praying for them? Write it down below.

MIND GAMES

Romans 12:2

Do not conform to the pattern of this world, but be transformed by the renewing of your mind. Then you will be able to test and approve what God's will is—his good, pleasing and perfect will.

2 Corinthians 10:5

We demolish arguments and every pretension that sets itself up against the knowledge of God, and we take captive every thought to make it obedient to Christ.

Romans 8:5-6

Those who live according to the flesh have their minds set on what the flesh desires; but those who live in accordance with the Spirit have their minds set on what the Spirit desires. The mind governed by the flesh is death, but the mind governed by the Spirit is life and peace.

1 Corinthians 2:16b

But we have the mind of Christ.

DEVO

Maybe you're like me and you can remember the very first pornographic images you saw. It's as if they were etched into the hard drive of the mind at such a deep level they can never be erased. And many of the images viewed thereafter seem to find their way into that repository as well. Then, when temptation hits, the vault is opened, the hard drive accessed, and a flood of memories come streaming into our consciousness. If only we could delete them and never have access again!

The reality is that we can. Well, we can't, but God can. God is in the business of rewiring minds and deleting sin-filled hard drives. The bible is very clear that transformation is partly a function of renewing our minds. One way we do that is by taking each thought captive and making it obedient to Christ. By the way, the language used in the Greek here is: *aichmalotizo*. The word actually means to bring under dominion by military force. Fighting the mind games won't be a walk in the park; it'll be an all-out war!

Unfortunately, the more we dwell on and think about the sinful, sexual things of life, the easier it becomes and more normal it feels to dwell on those things. It is self-perpetuating.

Thankfully, the inverse is true too.

The good news is that our mind can be changed, and even physiologically, our neural-chemistry can literally be changed. The pathways in our brains that transmit messages and images can be rewired so that we crave sexual stimulation less. When we partner with the Holy Spirit we can begin to develop the mind of Christ.

 SELF

What do you know needs to be deleted from the hard drive of your mind?

When you consider that changing our thoughts and fantasies will be a war, what does it stir in you? Do you consider that a challenge? Or do you sense resignation already within yourself?

What does it mean to you to be "transformed by the renewing of your mind"? How does that look in day-to-day life?

⚙ TAKE ACTION

We're going to practice a visualization exercise that will take five to ten minutes. You'll want to be somewhere quiet to do this. We'll come back to this exercise later in the book and combine it with our ReWired action step.

Read through the process below, commit it memory, then try it.

Begin by closing your eyes and taking a moment to clear your mind. Take a couple deep breaths then start to focus. Picture yourself packaging those sexual thoughts somehow: wadding up a piece of paper, filling a trash bag or cardboard box. It could be a small package or a dump-truck load. Next picture Jesus, alive, on the cross. Not dead, but alive and able to converse with you. See the scene vividly; what is happening in the background, the smell, the atmosphere, the people, the sky. Then visualize yourself placing your package at the foot of the cross. Along with the imagery of willfully putting it there, direct your mind's eye to look down at the ground to place the item, and then to look up to see Christ, the embodiment of grace, who oversees all. What would you say to Jesus and what He would say to you in the transaction? Let your mind engage this . . . what would He say to you?

Take a minute to acknowledge what you feel as you interact with Him there, and what you envision Him saying to you.

What was that visualization like for you? What did you say? What did Jesus say?

🙏 GOD

Prayerfully ask God to begin erasing the hard drive of your mind. Thank Him for neural plasticity, and the reality that our minds can change for the better. Invite Him to show you what He desires your mind to be set upon.

 OTHERS

Share with other men what you believe needs to be erased from your mind. Also, talk to them about they can help you in the battle for your mind.

Discuss what the visualization was like for you. Did you try it more than once, and if so, did anything change? Talk them through what you said, what He said, etc. Then commit to them that you'll be accountable to consistently place that package at the foot of the cross.

REWIRED

Philippians 4:8 (MSG)

Summing it all up, friends, I'd say you'll do best by filling your minds and meditating on things true, noble, reputable, authentic, compelling, gracious—the best, not the worst; the beautiful, not the ugly; things to praise, not things to curse.

DEVO

It is not enough to simply attempt to stop our sinful sexual thoughts. We must take it a step further in order to retrain our brains for holiness. The bible is clear on how we do this, and in the verse for this devo God specifically tells us what to focus our attention on. Things that are noble, reputable and beautiful are things that remind us of God and his goodness. They remind us of sweet things and good times, and they solicit warm emotions.

When we activate our sexuality, we are tapping into emotions like love, acceptance, comfort, euphoria, peace and belonging. We can connect to the same wiring and thus activate those same emotions by dwelling on specific memories. Think of some of the best times of your life; memorable moments where it felt like time slowed down and you could really take it in. Perhaps it was the birth of a child, a camping trip with friends, seeing a family member succeed at something, or it could be the moment you gave your life to Christ. When you dwell on these memories, they lead to warm feelings, but not sexual thoughts. And that's exactly what we're aiming for here!

We have the chance to change our brains and use our minds for good not evil, for redemption not destruction. The more we focus on thoughts that are pure, authentic, compelling and reputable, the more we develop the mind of Christ.

SELF

When temptation thoughts hit do you simply try to get rid of them, or do you actually dwell on something else?

Take some time to reflect on what memories fit Philippians 4:8 for you. It could be a memory of family members, of a fishing trip, of a particular place or time in your life. It could also be Scripture or a particular image of Jesus. In order to work effectively, these memories have to be vivid and clear in our minds.

Begin thinking about what memories will work as replacement thoughts for you.

 GOD

Invite God into the rewiring process. God is in the business of rewiring minds; ask Him to help rewire yours. Specifically, ask God to show you what in your world qualifies as noble, reputable, and compelling.

⚙ TAKE ACTION

This is where we integrate last weeks' visualization exercise. Every time we are tempted, there is an opportunity to take those thoughts captive and make them obedient to Christ. In other words, package them up and surrender them at the foot of the cross. Then, instead of dwelling on that old stuff, we have to use replacement thoughts. We intentionally focus our minds on memories that are beautiful, noble, and reputable. This process will result in a change in our brains physiologically as well as our minds spiritually.

Write down two memories that will function as your replacement thoughts.

Replacement Thought #1:

Replacement Thought #2:

When we take ourselves through the visualization exercise described in the previous chapter we are actually, literally, neurologically rewiring our brains for Godliness. Unfortunately, every time we've dwelt on fantasy and sexual thoughts we have wired our brains toward over-stimulation and hyper-sexualization. Now, every single time you are tempted, you have the chance to rewire your brain for health and holiness. What an opportunity!

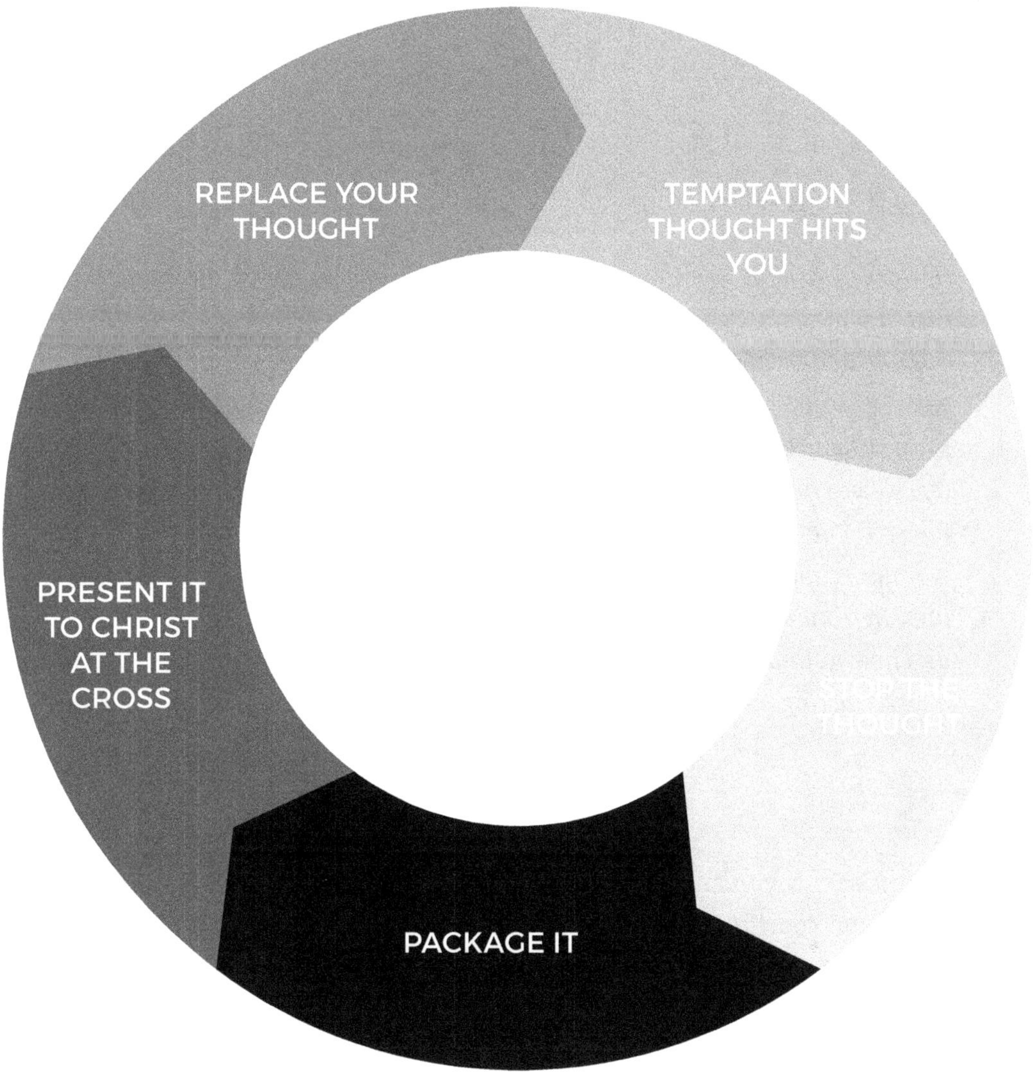

Diagram (cycle):
- TEMPTATION THOUGHT HITS YOU
- STOP THE THOUGHT
- PACKAGE IT
- PRESENT IT TO CHRIST AT THE CROSS
- REPLACE YOUR THOUGHT

 OTHERS

Talk to your connections about your replacement thoughts. Give them permission to speak into what those thoughts are and if they fit the bill. Be accountable for employing those thoughts regularly, each day. Report on this as a part of your check-in with them.

SELF-AWARE

Luke 8:43-48 (MSG)

In the crowd that day there was a woman who for twelve years had been afflicted with hemorrhages. She had spent every penny she had on doctors but not one had been able to help her. She slipped in from behind and touched the edge of Jesus' robe. At that very moment her hemorrhaging stopped. Jesus said, "Who touched me?" When no one stepped forward, Peter said, "But Master, we've got crowds of people on our hands. Dozens have touched you." Jesus insisted, "Someone touched me. I felt power discharging from me." When the woman realized that she couldn't remain hidden, she knelt trembling before him. In front of all the people, she blurted out her story—why she touched him and how at that same moment she was healed. Jesus said, "Daughter, you took a risk trusting me, and now you're healed and whole. Live well, live blessed!"

DEVO

Picture the scene: you and several thousand of your closest friends filing out of a professional sporting event, making your way down the stairs and escalators towards the exits. The atmosphere is exciting and the crowd of people talking and recounting plays creates a roar though the corridors. The chaotic, cattle herd-like flow of the crowd causes your personal space to be invaded on all sides and you are bumped and jostled along the way. Can you imagine the scene if you were to yell out, "Everyone stop! Someone just touched me!"

Would anyone listen? Would the crowd stop moving and the corridor become silent? Probably not. Everyone expects the jostling of the crowd.

There was a difference, however, in the touch that Jesus experienced. That touch was more profound. Healing happened when the person touched Him, and He knew it. He was keenly aware that this particular interaction was different than someone simply bumping into Him. It connected to a place inside Him, at a heart level, even a soul level. In His infinite self-awareness He acknowledged it.

"Power has gone out from me," He said. In other words, "this interaction affected me, as well as the person who came in contact with me. Things are not the same as prior to this touch!" Amongst the jostling of the crowd, Jesus was able to sense a very tender moment and a powerful transaction. We, like Jesus, must develop a self-awareness that enables us to recognize when we are impacted by people around us. Likewise, that self-awareness allows us to experience when people find a little bit of healing by interacting with us. We become a conduit of God's grace to other people.

Without self-awareness, we unfortunately may think we are merely bumping into people along the crowded corridors of life.

 SELF

How well do you know yourself, especially how you are impacted by interactions with other people? Do you recognize when they energize you? What about when they drain you?

When was the last time your interaction with someone seemed to provide them a little bit of healing? If you can think of a time, how did it make you feel. Did it change anything in you? If you can't think of a time, why do you think that is?

🙏 GOD

Write a prayer asking God to develop your sense of awareness. Ask Him to amplify those moments where bumping into someone is more than jostling in a crowd. Thank Him for any encouragement you've received from bumping into someone else.

 OTHERS

Take a moment to reflect on your sphere of influence. Who do you come in contact with regularly? Are there any encouraging words you could share with someone the next time you bump into them? Ask your accountability partners to help you commit to intentionally sharing with that person.

⚙ TAKE ACTION

It's time to take action. Practicing self-awareness, who do you sense might need encouraging words? Identify that person and prayerfully commit to bumping into them. Decide on a time frame for trying to make that interaction happen. May a bit of healing happen, for both of you. *Disclaimer - do not include people in this exercise that might be a part of your acting out. So if you've had physical or emotional affairs, leave women out of it. If you've struggled with same sex attraction, do not include men who you think might struggle that same way. You get the picture.*

Who is it?

What is your deadline to follow through?

HANDPICKED

> **John 6:70-71 (MSG)**
>
> *Jesus responded, "Haven't I handpicked you, the Twelve? Still, one of you is a devil!" He was referring to Judas, son of Simon Iscariot. This man—one from the Twelve!—was even then getting ready to betray him.*

DEVO

Judas was handpicked by Jesus to be a follower. We don't know when he made the fateful decision to betray his leader. All we know is that he did, and he became a glaring example of how to blow up our lives. So often the Scriptures about Judas are the proof text for betrayal, for deceit, and for backstabbing. But within the story is also an incredible example of love and grace.

Think about it—Jesus knew Judas would betray Him. BUT HE HANDPICKED HIM ANYWAY! Jesus called him a "devil" in this passage; the original Greek word here was *diabolos*. The meaning of the word is "to oppose the cause of God." Jesus wasn't calling Judas "Satan" so much as He was using a word that would shine light on Judas' current heart status and the choices he was making. So let's get this straight: Jesus handpicked the man whom He knew would betray Him and whom would oppose the cause of God the Father.

If Jesus had mercy on the guy who would ultimately get Him killed, don't you think he could have mercy on us? You need to know that you've been handpicked. You've been selected based on no merit of your own. Loved in spite of your bad behavior. Graced in spite of some future bad behavior. Jesus knows our past, present, and future; the Father forgives it; and we are free to live in light of Grace.

SELF

Have you heard a sermon where Judas was used as the example of what not to do? Have you heard a sermon about the grace of Jesus hanging out with Judas anyway? How does viewing the story through this second lens give you a different view of Judas—and of your own sins against Jesus?

Have you ever thought about the reality of being handpicked by God, in spite of the fact that we'll betray Him? What do you feel and think when you consider this?

Is it hard to believe that God's grace won't run out? Why or why not?

 **GOD**

Thank the Lord for being handpicked, chosen in spite of bad behavior, dearly loved simply by nature of being created in His image.

 OTHERS

Talk to your people about the idea of both Judas and us being handpicked by God. See what they think about it. How do they feel when they consider that we're all one bad decision away from being Judas ourselves?

LONGING

> **Isaiah 55:2**
>
> *Why spend money on what is not bread, and your labor on what does not satisfy?*
>
> **John 4:13-14 (MSG)**
>
> *Jesus said, "Everyone who drinks this water will get thirsty again and again. Anyone who drinks the water I give will never thirst—not ever. The water I give will be an artesian spring within, gushing fountains of endless life."*

DEVO

As we begin to understand ourselves and our sexual integrity issues better, we should begin to recognize that we're longing for something. We're longing for more than the act of sex, the thrill of the hunt, and the relief of release. We're searching for something more profound than intimacy with another human. We are thirsting for something at a soul level that any present libation is entirely inept to quench. I'll say it a different way: we are thirsty for something so deep that only Living Water can satisfy. We are hungry for a relational, intimate connection where our value is confirmed and affirmed.

The prophet Isaiah says we eat bread that is empty and labor for what does not satisfy. Jesus says we drink from wells that will run dry. If we examine our lives and our behavior of sexually acting out, we experientially know they are right. It's empty. We're empty. And the next bite or drink only satisfies for a fleeting moment. Isn't that your experience? It certainly is mine. Acting out sexually never actually satisfies.

I would submit that what we're really searching for is a tangible, experiential, real encounter with the Living God and His son Jesus. If we boil it down, it is God or nothing. If He doesn't show up, we're only going to sink down. If He isn't real to us, we'll continue running to what feels real to us. If He won't speak the words of affirmation we so desperately yearn to hear, we'll find someone who will. And we'll likely sexualize it. Even if we have to pay for it. Even if we have to demean, belittle, and objectify ourselves and someone else in the process.

Isn't it time to find our satisfaction in Jesus?

SELF

Pick two words to describe what you are searching for. Perhaps it is Love, Acceptance, Significance, Desirability, Respect, Fulfillment, Happiness, or Joy. Write those two words down below.

Word 1:

Word 2:

GOD

Begin to pray for God to show you how He can deliver what you are looking for. Ask Him to speak directly to those two words. If you've not experienced those things from Him, ask him to show you why. Ask Him to connect you with people in your life who can be "Jesus with skin on" to communicate His love to you.

OTHERS

Talk with your accountability partners about the two words you came up with.

Why those words? What happens when you don't have those needs met?

How do you respond to situations in life that tap into those words? How can the people you trust be helpful to fulfill those words?

TO WHOM

> **John 6:66-68**
>
> *From this time many of his disciples turned back and no longer followed him. "You do not want to leave too, do you?" Jesus asked the Twelve. Simon Peter answered him, "Lord, to whom shall we go? You have the words of eternal life."*

DEVO

The scene leading up to this verse is challenging. People are arguing about Jesus' point of origin—Heaven. He ends up making bold proclamations about himself and his ability to provide sustenance forever. He asserts that he can provide life everlasting if people will only digest what he is saying and drink in his truth.

The disciples are stunned by the "hard teaching" (John 6:60) and begin to debate what it means. Some followers hit the eject button and leave. Jesus confronts the rest of them as if to say, "Well, are you in or are you out?" Here Peter makes a sobering statement of surrender. When confronted by Jesus about his commitment, he doesn't make a case or an argument for being a committed follower. He simply says there is no alternative.

"Lord, to whom shall we go?"

If not YOU then who? Peter is communicating a stark reality that if not Jesus, there is nobody worthy of following.

No one has the authority to save, heal, change, deliver, redeem, encourage, convict, confront, disciple, or lead the way Jesus does.

👤 SELF

We must ask ourselves: Have we made the conscious acknowledgment that there is no other way? If not, when the teaching gets hard, we may just hit the eject button. Have you decided that the only person worthy of your deepest affinity and affection is Jesus Christ?

When times are tough, to what or whom do you turn that does not satisfy? Maybe it's food, sex, money, power, profession or physique?

 ## GOD

Prayerfully surrender what or whom you turn to, instead of God, when things get difficult. Here is an example prayer:

"God, I surrender self-help to you. I realize that no amount of reading, no amount of new insight, no new philosophy will ultimately help me change. I acknowledge that you, above all else, are the sole source of change. Would you please cause me to realize when I'm relying more on self-help than on your help."

 **OTHERS**

Talk with your connections about the things you run to when times are tough. What do you look to and why?

Talk to them about their determination that Jesus is the only one worthy of their deepest affinity. How does that play out in their life? How do they keep that in focus?

MY PERSONAL MISSION STATEMENT

CLEAN CLOTHES

> **Zechariah 3:4 (MSG)**
>
> *Joshua, standing before the angel, was dressed in dirty clothes. The angel spoke to his attendants, "Get him out of those filthy clothes," and then said to Joshua, "Look, I've stripped you of your sin and dressed you up in clean clothes.*
>
> **Isaiah 61:10 (MSG)**
>
> *I will sing for joy in God, explode in praise from deep in my soul! He dressed me up in a suit of salvation, he outfitted me in a robe of righteousness.*

DEVO

It is imperative for us to understand our righteousness. If we don't understand this foundational principle, we will struggle mightily through the rest of our journey towards sexual integrity. We are righteous. Not by our works, not by our looks, not by our bank accounts, not by our church attendance, not by our charitable donations, not by our behaviors, not by our eloquent prayers.

Only by the grace of God in Jesus.

You see, in accepting Christ our filthy rags were removed. The stench of sexual sin—past, present and future—was taken away. And it's not by anything we can do for ourselves. These verses clearly depict our re-dressing being the work of God and the heavenly hosts. We have been robed in righteousness and dressed in clean clothes. When we accept Christ, His righteousness is imputed to us. It's in us. It's on us. Nothing can remove it from us. You have to accept that in the middle of your acting out, in the midst of a porn session, in the intoxicating delusion of another affair, God sees you as clean.

As odd as it may be to imagine, He looks at you like a groom gazes at his bride on their wedding day. He loves you. He is grieved by your behavior, but He infinitely loves your being. You are righteous!

🧍 SELF

We're all familiar with the terribly shameful feeling of having just acted out again; wearing filthy rags. But are you familiar with the feeling of being clean and robed in righteousness? Describe a time when you experienced being clean, covered in Christ and free of guilt and shame. Maybe it was when you first gave your life to Christ, or perhaps when you were a child. Reflect on what it felt like to be released from shame and condemnation—and imagine how it might feel to have that again.

GOD

Pray a very simple prayer to God, in your own conversational way, asking Him to help you fully acknowledge and experience the righteousness He's already given you. Ask Him to help you see yourself the way He sees you. Invite Him to give you a picture that depicts your right standing with Him.

⚙ TAKE ACTION

Read Isaiah 61 below from The Message (MSG).

> **Isaiah 61**
> *Announce Freedom to All Captives*
>
> **1-7** The Spirit of God, the Master, is on me
>   because God anointed me.
> He sent me to preach good news to the poor,
>   heal the heartbroken,
> Announce freedom to all captives,
>   pardon all prisoners.
> God sent me to announce the year of his grace—
>   a celebration of God's destruction of our enemies—
>   and to comfort all who mourn,
> To care for the needs of all who mourn in Zion,
>   give them bouquets of roses instead of ashes,
> Messages of joy instead of news of doom,
>   a praising heart instead of a languid spirit.
> Rename them "Oaks of Righteousness"
>   planted by God to display his glory.
> They'll rebuild the old ruins,
>   raise a new city out of the wreckage.
> They'll start over on the ruined cities,
>   take the rubble left behind and make it new.
> You'll hire outsiders to herd your flocks
>   and foreigners to work your fields,
> But you'll have the title "Priests of God,"
>   honored as ministers of our God.
> You'll feast on the bounty of nations,
>   you'll bask in their glory.
> Because you got a double dose of trouble
>   and more than your share of contempt,
> Your inheritance in the land will be doubled
>   and your joy go on forever.
> **8-9** "Because I, God, love fair dealing

> *and hate thievery and crime,*
> *I'll pay your wages on time and in full,*
>
> *and establish my eternal covenant with you.*
> *Your descendants will become well-known all over.*
> *Your children in foreign countries*
> *Will be recognized at once*
> *as the people I have blessed."*
> **10-11** *I will sing for joy in God,*
> *explode in praise from deep in my soul!*
> *He dressed me up in a suit of salvation,*
> *he outfitted me in a robe of righteousness,*
> *As a bridegroom who puts on a tuxedo*
> *and a bride a jeweled tiara.*
> *For as the earth bursts with spring wildflowers,*
> *and as a garden cascades with blossoms,*
> *So the Master, God, brings righteousness into full bloom*
> *and puts praise on display before the nations.*

What stands out to you about this passage? How does it relate to your life?

 **OTHERS**

Discuss righteousness with your connections. What does it mean to be declared "righteous"? Do you agree or disagree that God sees you as robed in righteousness, as a groom sees his bride on the wedding day? Talk about how the Isaiah 61 passage relates to this idea.

INSTINCT

Jude 1:10 (MSG)

But these people sneer at anything they can't understand, and by doing whatever they feel like doing—living by animal instinct only—they participate in their own destruction.

DEVO

Some things we just know are very dangerous if misused—alcohol is an obvious example. But it is easy to write off the dangers of something that is instinctual, because it seems so natural, so simple, so expected. Yet in order to live well and honor God, we have to learn to contain those instinctual impulses.

Consider food; eating is instinctual, isn't it? We all know the dangers of overeating or eating really poorly, though: diabetes, stroke, heart attack, etc.

Same with sex; seems pretty instinctual too, right? But if we're honest, we've misused our sexuality in ways that can be dangerous too. We've engaged in acts we swore we would never commit, with people we never imagined, at times and places we would otherwise never go.

Too often I hear men express their "high sex drive" as the reason they act out sexually with pornography, masturbation, and even affairs. "It's natural for me to want to have sex," they say. Then, when coached or guided on containing those instinctual impulses and delaying sexual gratification, they get defensive, argumentative, and angry. In other words, they sneer at the advice.

Perhaps Jude was speaking to us when this was Scripture written, encouraging us to look deeper than our animal instincts.

Might our lives be different, and our relationship with God be different, if we tried to acknowledge our natural, instinctual impulses as both physical and spiritual? If we'll allow it, our natural instincts can lead us in two ways; 1) to act in a physical way, or 2) to act in a spiritual way.

The urge to eat can prompt us to find food for nourishment of our bodies. It can also be a prompt for us to seek spiritual nourishment, too. That's partly why we see that fasting can be such a spiritually enriching experience. The same can be true of sex. Sexual desire can be a prompt to engage intimately with another human, and by the same token, perhaps it can signal our need to engage intimately with our Creator.

Just because something is instinctual doesn't mean we know how to fulfill the desire appropriately, healthily, or in a God-honoring way. We have to be intentional to do so. That requires prayer, and honestly assessing to what end we're allowing these impulses to lead us.

 SELF

In what ways have you misused "natural" or "instinctual" things in your life? What have your heard or been taught lately that you sneer at simply because (if you're honest) you simply don't understand?

If every hunger pang and every sexual temptation were a prompt that you acted on to drive you into deeper relationship with God, would your life be any different? How and why?

🙏 GOD

Prayerfully ask God to show how you misuse instinctual things. Ask for help to fulfill desires appropriately and in a spiritually enriching way. Invite Him to help you grow more humble and receptive to things you don't understand.

OTHERS

Talk with your connections about how you can intentionally stretch yourself to learn about things you don't understand. Do this especially as it pertains to sex/sexuality. Write down their suggestions.

⚙ TAKE ACTION

The following books have challenged me to take a different perspective on my sexual impulses and how I act upon instincts. Consider picking up one or two of them. Perhaps they will shed a new light for you as well.

Anatomy of the Soul: Surprising Connections between Neuroscience and Spiritual Practices That Can Transform Your Life and Relationships
by Curt Thompson (Tyndale).

When Good Men are Tempted
by Bill Perkins (Zondervan).

Wired for Intimacy: How Pornography Hijacks the Male Brain
by William M. Struthers (IVP Books).

A QUICK CHECK-IN

Have you been reciting the Romans 8:1 verse? If not, consider this your reminder! (See page 9 for the *Not Condemned* devo).

> **Romans 8:1**
>
> *Therefore, there is now no condemnation for those who are in Christ Jesus.*

Recite Romans 8:1 aloud three times, personalizing the language. (e.g. "Therefore I, (*your name here*), am not condemned, because I, (*your name here*) am in Christ Jesus.")

PROTECTION

2 Samuel 22:31

As for God, his way is perfect:
The Lord's word is flawless;
he shields all who take refuge in him.

Psalm 46:1

God is our refuge and strength,
an ever-present help in trouble.

Psalm 62:7

My salvation and my honor depend on God;
he is my mighty rock, my refuge.

DEVO

Have you ever considered what temptations, trials, or tribulations God has already protected you from? Ones you never even felt or experienced? Have you reflected on the ones where He delivered you from the very midst? How many times has He saved you from yourself? These unseen instances are probably too great to count.

The visible instances are often easy to forget; the invisible ones even easier to miss. Yet we cannot underestimate His sovereignty. We cannot overestimate His love. We have His word that we're protected. By His outstretched arm and mighty hand He protects His people. It may not seem like it today, but He is busy at the work of protecting you. Instead of spending time asking questions about why He won't deliver you from your sin, reframe your perspective and attempt to see where He may already saving you from the magnitude of it.

When I reflect on my sexual addiction and all the damage I did, I can also see how much worse it could have been. There were so many opportunities for me to blow up my life with greater magnitude and collateral damage, and God was faithful to protect me from myself. There were near misses with another woman's husband, close calls with scams and setups, and the possibility of getting arrested. There but for the grace of God go I.

Perhaps even today God is protecting you. I suspect if you look for it you'll see it.

 SELF

Identify a few examples of God protecting you from yourself. In what ways might there have been more damage had He not intervened?

 GOD

Earnestly thank God for showing up as He has. Ask for Him to show you how He's been protecting you. Pray for deliverance from sin, and thank Him for the work He is already doing in you.

TAKE ACTION

Spend some time today considering the "what-ifs," and looking for places where God might be at work protecting you. It may be in traffic, at work, at home, with your sexual temptation, with your anger or passivity, or even with your finances.

OTHERS

Talk about those instances you identified where God has likely protected you from yourself and the potential collateral damage you've forgone.

OBEDIENCE

> **Deuteronomy 8:6**
>
> *Observe the commands of the LORD your God, walking in obedience to him and revering him.*

DEVO

We are, by nature, disobedient. Our bent is towards independence and individuality. Our brokenness as a result of original sin has created a tendency in us to go our own way and to disobey the authority of God. In sexual sin, we are outwardly defiant. We are looking our Father in the face and saying, "I know you think you know what is best for my life and my sexuality, but I don't trust you. I trust ME." We become very skilled at ignoring God's commands, rationalizing why we don't or shouldn't follow them, and then behaving in a way that thumbs our nose at Him. We all know, experientially, that repetitive disobedience makes each subsequent defiance a little easier.

It is important to remember that the reverse is true too! The more we choose to move into obedience and revering God, the easier it becomes to obey His commands. The less you act out sexually the easier it will become to avoid acting out sexually. Remember talking about this back in Mind Games and ReWired? We can actually change our brains and make it easier to choose the right course each time we do it.

How do we begin choosing what is right? First, it's important to remember that obedience is not about avoiding some bad behavior for the sake of good behavior. Obedience is a response to the love of a Father God who deeply cares about His kids. When we begin to accept that God's commands aren't intended to kill our fun but instead to bolster our joy, we'll be more likely to obey. Obedience isn't about what you do or don't do so much as it is a response to who God is and whom you are to Him.

 **SELF**

Besides sexual integrity, in what areas of your life is it most difficult to obey God? What's your take on God's requiring obedience of us: to kill our joy or bolster it?

What were you taught growing up about obedience—was it a response to the rules or a response to relationships? Were you obedient out of honor and reverence or simply consequence avoidance?

 **GOD**

Are there specific areas in which you're holding back from fully obeying Him?

Prayerfully ask God in which areas of your life He would like you to respond in obedience. Ask for the boldness, willingness, and humility to follow through even when your bent is to defy Him.

⚙ TAKE ACTION

What do you believe God is asking of you with regard to sexual sin? Hint: simply answering "stop doing X" is not a sufficient answer. God is likely calling you to some concrete, actionable steps that will lead you into full obedience in this area. Here are some common steps I see men take: changing jobs, committing to counseling, going to an Every Mans Battle workshop, telling your affair partner it is over, blocking Craigslist with your internet filter, choosing to stop going to lunch with people you lust after.

Decide what it is and commit to taking that step or steps.

 OTHERS

Deciding where we need to be obedient is tough, and following through on it is even more difficult—even with the best of intentions. Tell your accountability partners about your commitment to taking this step. Let them know specifically what obedient action you'll take. Then, touch base with them periodically about your follow-through on it.

DAILY MANNA

> **Exodus 16:4**
>
> *Then the LORD said to Moses, "I will rain down bread from heaven for you. The people are to go out each day and gather enough for that day."*
>
> **Exodus 16:15-16**
>
> *Moses said to them, "It is the bread the Lord has given you to eat. This is what the LORD has commanded: 'Everyone is to gather as much as they need.'"*
>
> **John 6:33**
>
> *For the bread of God is the bread that comes down from heaven and gives life to the world.*

DEVO

Too often we look for a quantifiable benchmark as an indication of our recovery/sanctification/progress. If we could just reach a week clean, month clean, or a year of not acting out or a decade of sobriety, somehow that would solidify our status. We would then be worthy of the freedom and righteousness we've already received. It's as if the present truth of our righteousness isn't real until some future reality (not acting out) is achieved that proves it. But when we employ this logic, we lose sight of the truth of God's sufficiency for today.

For the Israelites wandering in the desert, God provided exactly what they needed to sustain them for the day. He instructed them to gather just enough for that day—promising that He would provide again for them the next day and the next.

Each day, He was enough.

Jesus relates Himself to the Old Testament manna by describing Himself as the Bread of Life. In effect, He's communicating that He is enough for us today. He'll sustain us: today.

Are you relying on him for that? Are you willing to risk Him not showing up? Or are you looking at your sobriety or the number of days that you've avoided acting out to be your deliverer—thinking that if you get enough consecutive days/weeks/months it'll be enough to sustain you? Newsflash—it won't. Nothing will be enough to sustain you. Except Him. Nothing. Just Him.

When this life is done and we have the gracious opportunity to meet the Savior, He won't be asking us how many days we were able to string together without acting out. He'll be asking whether we were sold out to a relationship with Him; day to day, week to week, month to month, year after year. Because He knows that a sustained relationship with Him will result in year-after-year sobriety.

SELF

What is manna—the thing that sustains you—in your life today? Perhaps your accountability partners, your friends, your wife, your church? Is it your job? Your finances? Or perhaps your addiction? Which of these are healthy or rely on, and which are not?

Read the sections of John 6:31-33 (MSG) below.

> **John 6:31-33**
> ***The Bread of Life***
>
> *"Show us what you can do. Moses fed our ancestors with bread in the desert. It says so in the Scriptures: 'He gave them bread from heaven to eat.'"*
>
> *Jesus responded, "The real significance of that Scripture is not that Moses gave you bread from heaven but that my Father is right now offering you bread from heaven, the real bread. The Bread of God came down out of heaven and is giving life to the world."*

What does it mean, to you personally, that the Father is offering you real bread, right now?

GOD

Thank God for His provision for today. Acknowledge His sovereignty over your life and ask Him to show you how to lean on Him. Ask Him to show you what manna looks like in real terms, today.

⚙ TAKE ACTION

Pick four different times throughout the day where you can take the first minute of the hour to thank God for your sobriety the hour before, and pray for His provision in the hour to come. For example, you might set an alarm in your phone or calendar for 9 a.m., 11 a.m., 2 p.m., and 6 p.m. Practice it each day this week.

Don't turn the page until you've actually set the reminders, written on post-it notes, or put it in your calendar!

OTHERS

Share with your connections about your take on John 6; what you saw, learned and what God has shown you.

Also, talk to them about the Take Action homework, your commitment to it, and then follow up on your experience of it. Invite them to do it with you.

SHAME DETOX

> **Isaiah 61:7**
>
> *Instead of your shame you will receive a double portion, and instead of disgrace you will rejoice in your inheritance.*

DEVO

We must learn to distinguish between conviction, shame, and guilt.

Conviction, which we could also call "Biblical shame," DRIVES ME TO GOD; it is a feeling and self-concept we experience when we engage an action that is sinful, or when we sinfully do not engage in an action we know we should. That sense of conviction is designed to point out our un-holiness, the state of our sanctification and how lacking it is compared to God. It is meant to help us recognize the depravity of our fallen state of humanity. Conviction should propel us to press in to what God wants to do in our lives and allow Him to change our character, the byproduct of which will be a change in behavior. Conviction points us toward true repentance, not just being sorry.

Shame DRIVES ME AWAY FROM GOD; it is a feeling and self-concept that is wholly fraudulent. It involves a deep, core belief that I am defective—not in the sense of our fallen humanity but in the sense of my personal identity. Shame tells us that the core of our soul, which God hand-crafted, is broken to a point of worthlessness. That God made a mistake with us. That maybe we aren't worth saving. That possibly God has given up on us and others likely will too. This sense of shame drives us to believe that we can somehow behave in a way that saves our being—an effort that ultimately proves futile. Shame says, "I AM a mistake, and I AM worthless, but maybe I can behave my way into BEING valuable." Shame does not come from the Holy Spirit, but from the Enemy.

Finally, *guilt* is simply an emotion we experience when we engage wrong behavior or do not engage right behavior. Whether by conscience or by the Holy Spirit, we experience a sense that the way we've behaved falls short. The guilty emotion is in place to motivate us to correct our behavior. Guilt says, "I MADE a mistake"—not "I AM a mistake."

 SELF

Have you considered how you talk to yourself? Reflect on what you say to yourself when you've made a mistake; especially when you've acted out. Chances are, you use shame messages to reprimand yourself—things like, "You're worthless" or "How could you do this again? You're a failure."

Identify the toxic shame messages in your life. Maybe you heard them growing up or as a young adult. Perhaps they are messages you tell yourself.

Now, consider what the truth is. God has delivered messages about our identity and worth through His word. He has spoken over us that we are valuable, loved, and righteous, no matter what we've done. Here are a couple of examples from Scripture that give us a window into how God feels about us.

> **Isaiah 43:1-4 (The Message)**
>
> *But now, God's Message,*
>   *the God who made you in the first place, Jacob,*
>   *the One who got you started, Israel:*
> *"Don't be afraid, I've redeemed you.*
>   *I've called your name. You're mine.*
> *When you're in over your head, I'll be there with you.*
>   *When you're in rough waters, you will not go down.*
> *When you're between a rock and a hard place,*
>   *it won't be a dead end—*
> *Because I am God, your personal God,*
>   *The Holy of Israel, your Savior.*
> *I paid a huge price for you:*
>   *all of Egypt, with rich Cush and Seba thrown in!*
> *That's how much you mean to me!*
>   *That's how much I love you!*
> *I'd sell off the whole world to get you back,*
>   *trade the creation just for you.*

> **1 John 3:1 (NIV)**
>
> *See what great love the Father has lavished on us, that we should be called children of God! And that is what we are!*

Now I want you to personalize it. Write down at least three truths about yourself that you can lean on when the shame messages feel overwhelming.

1.)

2.)

3.)

🙏 GOD

Begin to prayerfully bring those shame messages to God, asking Him to refute the lies and deposit truth in your heart and mind. Remember, the foot of the cross is a No Shame Zone.

OTHERS

Once you've identified the toxic shame messages, tell your accountability partners about them. Let them in on the way you talk to yourself, especially these negative messages.

Also, talk to them about what message you need consistently from them to help refute the lies. Ask them if they have messages of their own that they rely on to help push away lies that creep in and cause shame. What words of truth can you speak to them when they need help offsetting toxic shame? Take notes below.

SELF-DEFEAT

James 1:14-15

...but each person is tempted when they are dragged away by their own evil desire and enticed. Then, after desire has conceived, it gives birth to sin; and sin, when it is full-grown, gives birth to death.

DEVO

Sometimes we're too quick to blame our temptation on the Devil and the culture we live in. Is it true that temptation arises from these sources—the devil tempting us through TV and movies with sexual content, easy access to pornography, a culture that encourages hooking up and sex with no strings attached. However, *oftentimes our temptation originates from within.*

It begins when we are dragged away and enticed. What does that mean? It means our focus shifts away from what matters most and we become distracted with what fulfills the least. Many of us have reels of old footage in our minds from past porn binges, affairs, strip clubs, and chat lines that we can recollect and thereby be enticed by. When we engage that footage and allow ourselves to fantasize about it, we are being dragged away; or to put it in context of the verse, we are dragging ourselves away. Where is that going to lead us?

We also experience temptation as a form of dealing with our emotions. Some of us have learned that emotions such as anger, insignificance, loneliness, rejection, fear, failure, and disappointment can be numbed and soothed by engaging sexual thoughts and actions. Unfortunately, it is easier to indulge in those unhealthy behaviors and medicate rather than to deal with the emotions appropriately. It was very difficult for me to accept this truth and to learn to deal with my emotions in healthy ways. It was especially difficult to learn how to process my emotions with other people. I wanted to keep it all bottled up and to myself. I didn't want to weigh anyone down with my junk. I wanted people to think I had it altogether, that I wasn't needy.

The truth is: we're all needy, and sometimes we have to get needy out loud.

Whether to numb feelings or to excite ourselves, when we act out sexually we are giving birth to sin, and ultimately that will give way to death. We have to take ownership for our self-temptation and be willing to engage our neediness—which will mean asking for help from others.

 SELF

In what ways do you tempt yourself, effectively dragging yourself away to be enticed?

Are there particular places you frequent where you know you are allowing yourself to be enticed? Perhaps restaurants, bars, events, work locations, etc?

What specific old footage do you still need to surrender?

 **GOD**

Repent and ask forgiveness from God for your self-temptation. Acknowledge to Him your desire to hang on to these old thoughts and ways of coping. Tell Him what specific footage you're ready to let go of.

 OTHERS

Talk with your connections about this self-temptation—what footage you replay in your head. Invite them to ask questions and give feedback on it. Ask them to pray for your willingness to surrender it. Be accountable for ongoing self-temptation. It will be hard to get so vulnerable, but chances are your friends want to be able to walk with you through this, and they will be glad to help you begin to surrender this baggage.

 TAKE ACTION

Go back and re-read the visualization exercise in the Mind Games devotional. Practice using it to get rid of the old footage.

THE DEVIL MADE ME DO IT

> **1 Peter 5:8**
>
> *Be alert and of sober mind. Your enemy the devil prowls around like a roaring lion looking for someone to devour.*
>
> **John 10:10**
>
> *The thief comes to steal, kill and destroy.*
>
> **Matthew 4:1**
>
> *Jesus was tempted by Satan.*

DEVO

In the last devo, Self-Defeat, we talked about how temptation can originate from within ourselves. Sometimes though it does not come from within, it comes from the Enemy. Just like it was for Jesus, it is Satan who presents us with opportunities to hijack God's will. And it can look pretty appetizing. Thankfully we have Jesus as a mentor who modeled how to refute temptation. It is interesting to note a few things about when He was tempted, to help set the stage.

First, Jesus' temptation came during His solo trip to the wilderness. Satan loves for men like us to be isolated and alone. He loves it when we don't have a solid community around us. That is when we're most vulnerable and exposed—the easiest time for Satan to get in and do his dirty work.

Second, it was immediately following Jesus' baptism in the Jordan river. This baptism was a celebratory event, inaugurating the ministry of Jesus. Satan will try to catch us off guard; sometimes immediately following a high point.

Third, it is also important to note that Satan appealed to Jesus when He legitimately needed something. Jesus' hunger was a real, felt need. Satan knows we are more vulnerable to short-circuit God's plan when we are in need—whether physically, emotionally, or spiritually.

Finally, Satan's temptation will always result in less than the best for our life and less than the utmost honor for God. If he can, Satan will try to tarnish God's reputation by coaxing us into accepting a fraudulent substitute that he knows will ultimately disappoint us. The hope being we'll look back at God and wonder why He let us down.

Now, with these things in mind, let's look at a few countermeasures Jesus employed during the attack.

1. He was prepared by prayer. We know Jesus was fasting, which in Biblical context is usually associated with prayer. Suffice it to say, Jesus was prayed up, ready for what might come at Him. *We have to be prayerfully prepared to take on what life and Satan bring at us.*

2. Jesus had a discerning ear towards the temptation. He was able to filter it against what He knew to be true about God and His nature. *We also must seek to know the nature of God,* such that when temptation offers us the opportunity to meet legitimate needs in illegitimate ways, we are able to discern the temptation and make a choice to turn to the correct path.

3. Jesus knew scripture and refuted Satan's twisting of it. *We have to know Scripture.* As a discipline, we must regularly be in the Word, chewing on it, digesting it, letting it penetrate our hearts and minds. It may even be helpful to choose particular pertinent verses and commit them to memory. Satan is crafty and knows Scripture too.

4. Jesus didn't enter into a debate with the Enemy. He simply refuted what was being thrown at him. Sometimes we want to entertain both sides of an argument; we can even rationalize how giving into a temptation might make sense! Before we get wrapped up in a debate with the Devil, *we have to shut down the conversation.*

👤 SELF

How can you incorporate Jesus' countermeasures into your everyday life?

When you consider the idea of being "prayed up" for life, what does it mean to you?

Can you identify times when you are most vulnerable because of isolation? If so, what steps can you take to prepare for the next time you are in that space?

TAKE ACTION

Start by simply taking six minutes out of your day to practice: *pray (one minute), read (two minutes),* and then *listen (three minutes).* The idea is to develop a rhythm of doing this multiple times each day.

Personally, I'd rather be doing any of these for short bursts than for long sittings. If that method doesn't work for you, engage in longer periods of reading, praying, and listening; but give the six-minute version a try to start. Everyone has six minutes somewhere in their day that they can manage to set aside for God.

🙏 GOD

Ask God to help you identify what Satan's offer is when you are tempted. Try to see what Satan is offering you that hijacks God's will for your life. Remember, his temptation will always result in less than the best for your life and less than utmost honor for God.

 OTHERS

Discuss why you think God allows us, along with His son, to be tempted. Also, talk about developing that 1x2x3 rhythm of praying, reading, and listening. How can they help you with that?

MY PERSONAL MISSION STATEMENT

REMINDERS

Deuteronomy 11:18-22

Fix these words of mine in your hearts and minds; tie them as symbols on your hands and bind them on your foreheads. Teach them to your children, talking about them when you sit at home and when you walk along the road, when you lie down and when you get up. Write them on the door frames of your houses and on your gates, so that your days and the days of your children may be many in the land the Lord swore to give your ancestors, as many as the days that the heavens are above the earth.

DEVO

The Israelites were a fickle people, weren't they? Slavery to freedom, then complaining that slavery was better. Moses today, a golden calf tomorrow. Manna today, then forgetting God's provision tomorrow. God knew they needed help to serve Him faithfully and consistently. He knew they were a little A.D.D. and forgot Him easily. He was devoted to helping them help themselves. By the way, if you believe the mantra, "God only helps those who help themselves" you might want to reread the entire Bible. The fundamental essence of God's love and Jesus Christ's death, burial, and resurrection is to take the initiative to restore us back to Him, as it is impossible for us to do this ourselves.

Anyway, knowing the Israelites would likely forget God's provision of freedom and His law, He urged them to talk about it often and to write it on their door frames and city gates. The idea is simply this: put reminders for yourself in the places you are most likely to see them. Every day, often multiple times a day, the Israelites would pass through the city gates and through the door frames of their houses and were sure to see the commands and reminders of the Lord there. We can heed this advice and apply this to our recovery and sanctification process as well. We can use visual cues to remind us of what God has done, what He is doing in our lives, who we are to Him, and what commands are near and dear to our hearts.

👤 SELF

What do you need to be consistently reminded of regarding your identity and your journey?

Name the places you see every day where a reminder might be helpful (ex: your phone, calendar, desk, bathroom mirror, dashboard).

 GOD

Ask God to help with your forgetfulness and fickleness. Ask Him to help you remember his deliverance, nearness, and commitment to you.

 **OTHERS**

Talk with your connections about the Take Action step that follows. Commit to follow through on putting up visual cues.

 TAKE ACTION

You've already identified the "door frames and city gates"; places in your life where you are most likely to see reminders. Now it's time to actually develop those reminders and implement them. Here are five things I urge you to write on notecards or type into your phone to use as visual cues:

1. Your personal mission statement from the first devo.

2. A Bible verse that speaks to you regarding your identity in Christ (ex: Ephesians 1, 1 Peter 2:9). Perhaps one of the statements you wrote down in the Shame Detox Devo?

3. A Bible verse that spurs you on towards sexual integrity. (ex: John 10:10)

4. A statement of truth about yourself. (ex: I have the Grace of God in my life)

5. A statement of truth about who God is. (ex: Deut 32:4, Titus 1:2)

RIPCORD

1 Corinthians 10:13

No temptation has seized you except what is common to man. And God is faithful; he will not let you be tempted beyond what you can bear. But when you are tempted, he will also provide a way out so that you can stand up under it.

DEVO

Temptation is guaranteed. A way out and the strength to bear the temptation is also guaranteed. I can tell you, in the midst of my addiction I saw no way out; no exits. But in hindsight, they were there all along the way. God was ever faithful, giving me ample opportunities to pull the ripcord. The problem was, I couldn't see them because they weren't what I would have chosen. God's commitment to us is unwavering; He will always provide a way out. And that way out will always be the best thing for us. It might not be what we want or what we would choose for ourselves, but it is ultimately for our good.

The night my wife, Shelley, confronted me about my infidelity was my way out. It was actually an extreme act of grace and mercy for God to lead her to the truth and then to give her the confidence to confront me. If I couldn't see the exits along the way, He knew it would require me slamming into a dead end.

Perhaps the same is true in your life? Maybe the computer crashing, the near miss at work, almost getting arrested, getting busted, etc. are all acts of extreme grace. God is beckoning you to pull the ripcord.

When temptation comes your way, you can count on God to offer you a way out. Search for it like your life depends on it.

It does.

 **SELF**

Are you aware of any opportunities God has given you to get out of temptation that you haven't taken?

How can you be more open to, and aware of, God's intervention in your times of temptation?

 GOD

Thank God that He will not allow you to be tempted beyond what you can handle. Ask Him to make the exits blatantly obvious in your life. Ask for the courage to take the off-ramp when you see it.

⚙ TAKE ACTION

I urge you to begin the habit of calling someone—an accountability partner or someone who may know some of your struggles—every single day. Not just text or email, not just voicemail. Actually talk every day for the next week and see how that practice intersects with temptation.

OTHERS

Calling an accountability partner can make for a great ripcord. The problem, though, is it takes practice to pull it. If you aren't in the habit of calling accountability partners regularly, it is highly unlikely you'll call in a time of need. Sometimes God's provision for getting out from temptation takes practice. Talk to your guys about the Take Action step in this devo, and if you haven't already, commit to calling them.

SELF-CONTROL

> **Proverbs 25:28**
>
> *Like a city whose walls are broken through*
>   *is a person who lacks self-control.*

DEVO

In a Biblical time when cities were attacked at the whim of an opposing empire, city walls were of paramount importance. A city without walls meant it was vulnerable to attack. Not only attack to be overtaken, but to be pillaged and plundered. There could never be a sense of security for the city's inhabitants. In all likelihood, there was a persistent fear instead of peace. In the same way, when a man lacks self-control, he is vulnerable to attacks from other people and the Enemy. He is likely going to experience life with a pervasive sense of fear and it is unlikely he'll find peace. For many men, the only place where they express feeling peace is in the medicated state of acting out sexually.

At the onslaught of another attack, a man without discipline will be overtaken like a city without any protective barrier. So how can we ward off such attacks? Self-control provides the first line of defense against the attacks we face. It protects us against the fiery arrows of a hyper-sexualized culture. It cannot be developed overnight, just like a city wall cannot be built overnight. However, with consistency and effort, your character can be formed to be a man of discipline and self-control.

SELF

In what areas of your life, even outside sexual integrity issues, do you struggle with self-control? Write them down as you think of them. Ex: candy, exercise, alcohol, gambling, stealing office supplies from work.

If you had to rate your overall self-control, where would it fall on a scale of one to ten?

1   2   3   4   5   6   7   8   9   10

We can begin to develop self control by practicing it in other areas of life. Sometimes we need to get a little momentum in small ways before we can utilize it in big ways. For example, we might begin with self control around food portions or spending/saving. Perhaps we practice with small ways we use our time, like spending 5 minutes of our lunch break praying rather than surfing sports articles.

In what area of life, in a small way, can you commit to practicing self control? Write it down here.

 **GOD**

Invite God into your self-control. Ask Him to empower and embolden you. Ask for his power to be made perfect in your weakness. Ask God to show you where the next layer of self-control needs to be developed in your life.

 OTHERS

Ask a couple of people close to you to rate your self-control on the ten-point scale. How does it line up with how you view yourself? Invite their suggestions on what you can do to improve self-control. Commit to them to be accountable for the small things of self-control this week.

COMFORT

> **2 Corinthians 1:3-4**
>
> *Praise be to the God and Father of our Lord Jesus Christ, the Father of compassion and the God of all comfort, who comforts us in all our troubles, so that we can comfort those in any trouble with the comfort we ourselves receive from God.*

DEVO

Have you ever noticed what it is that connects you deeply to someone else's story about God's work in their lives? I'm not talking about the casual, cognitive connection to a shared experience; I'm talking about the deep, emotional, empathic kinship. Chances are you're pulled in by one or both of these things: their pain or their hope. Sometimes it is both. You can relate to the pain that person has experienced because of your own story, and you long for the hope that comes from the way their story turned out. What if God's purpose for comforting us is not simply to soothe our own pain but also to make us co-laborers in His plan of comforting hurting people? What if it's also about creating a point in our story that someone else can connect to? And perhaps in that connection they can catch a glimpse of Him and a glimmer of hope.

Some of us are selfish in our desire for comfort. We long for God to comfort us by setting us free from our addictions simply so we can be free. It has nothing to do with helping someone else get free. I can tell you that was true of me. I prayed over and over again for God to show up, but I really just wanted Him to show for my sake. I didn't want to feel guilty anymore. I didn't want to be the bad husband. I didn't want to be the hypocrite. I didn't want to be "that" guy. And the last thing I was interested in was helping others. I needed to get on with my agenda for life. It wasn't until my prayers shifted to total surrender that God intervened. I sometimes wonder if the reason He seemed to be withholding comfort for so long was this very thing: that in His sovereignty he knew I would hoard His comfort and it would be wasted on me. Perhaps He knew that, until I truly had to surrender everything to Him and His plan, I wouldn't use it for others' sake.

I urge you to begin thinking about how you would use the comfort God gives you to comfort others. Start considering how your pain and hope can be the very point of connection someone else needs to see a glimpse of the Living God.

SELF

In what ways has God comforted you? Do you ever feel like He is holding out on you?

🙏 GOD

Pray for comfort, in His way and on His terms. See what comes to mind when you pray for it. Ask God to show you who needs your comfort, as a conduit of His divine comfort.

OTHERS

How can your connections comfort you? And how can you comfort them? What does that mean, in practical terms, and is comfort different for your accountability partners versus your wife (if you're married)? If so, how?

IDOL TIME

> **Colossians 3:5**
>
> *Put to death, therefore, whatever belongs to your earthly nature: sexual immorality, impurity, lust, evil desires and greed, which is idolatry.*

DEVO

This verse, written by Paul, is a linear expression of sexual immorality. In effect, Paul starts with the leaves on the tree and strategically works his way to the roots. The Greek word for sexual immorality is *porneaia*, which means illicit sexual intercourse. That same word is also a metaphor for idol worship. Ultimately, what Paul is saying is that our sexual acting-out behavior is rooted in idolatry.

It is giving our attention, affection, and affinity to something other than our Heavenly Father.

When we do this, we end up serving ourselves rather than Him. And, in the end, we end up putting our hope and expectations in something that can never ultimately satisfy. We're setting ourselves up to be hurt and disappointed. I love what Scott Nickell, teaching pastor at Flatirons Community Church in Lafayette, Colorado, often says: "When good things become ultimate things, ultimately good things become destructive things."[1] He's describing what happens when we make an idol out of something, especially sexual sin.

The idea of putting sexual immorality to death in our lives is not an expectation that we stop being sexual; that's something God beautifully created. Instead we are called to recognize the ultimate place sex has taken in our hearts and minds, to acknowledge the destruction this has caused, and to deprive it of the power

---

[1] In case you're interested, here's where you can check out Flatirons Church: **www.flatironschurch.com/messages**

it has over us. Paul is saying we are to put sex in it's rightful place—taking it off the pedestal of our lives and putting God first.

Did you know that sex and sexual acting out have no power over you? I know sometimes it feels like it does, like if we don't act out and release that we'll explode, but truthfully sex has absolutely zero power over you. God is greater than your sexual desire. As long as your worship—your attention, affection, and affinity—is toward sexual things, you will remain subject to its whims. Only when we smash the idol and turn our eyes to focus on the true Living God will we find the freedom we long for.

 SELF

Have you acknowledged that sexual sin is idolatry? Have you admitted giving your attention, affection, and affinity to it?

Is there anything else—work, exercise, money—that you currently give your attention and affection to that might be hurting you?

Who, besides God, rightly needs some of your attention, affection, and affinity today? Not to be idolized, but to be honored.

If you allow yourself to dream for a minute, who could potentially be impacted for the better if you dismantled sexual idolatry in your life?

 **GOD**

Ask God to help you realize when you are bowing at the altar of idolatry again. Ask for the Holy Spirit to intervene and direct your affinity, affection, and attention towards the cross.

 OTHERS

Talk with your connections about idolatry the things you put above God. Talk about who in your life needs you to be fully present with them. Discuss how those people could benefit from your affinity, affection, and attention, and how to give it to them in a way that still keeps God in the ultimate place of honor.

Talk about what it would mean to smash the idol of sexual immorality. How does that look in practicality?

TRAVEL LIGHTER

Proverbs 28:13

Whoever conceals their sins does not prosper, but the one who confesses and renounces them finds mercy.

1 John 1:9

If we confess our sins, he is faithful and just and will forgive us our sins and purify us from all unrighteousness.

Psalm 32:3-5

When I kept silent, my bones wasted away through my groaning all day long. For day and night your hand was heavy on me; my strength was sapped as in the heat of summer. Then I acknowledged my sin to you and did not cover up my iniquity. I said, "I will confess my transgressions to the Lord." And you forgave the guilt of my sin.

James 5:16a

Therefore confess your sins to each other and pray for each other so that you may be healed.

DEVO

I travel at least once a month, and it never ceases to amaze me how much junk people drag through the airport. Have you seen these folks? They have two bags with the straps wrapped around their neck and three bags in tow, one of those bulging at the seams because its stuffed with who knows what. Plus, they have a "carry on" that wouldn't fit in the back of my 4Runner much less an overhead bin. And the worst part, it's almost inevitable that they'll be in front of me in the security line. Ugh.

I just want to say, "Get rid of some of that stinking baggage!"

I wonder if sometimes that's what God wants to say to us!

Confession is just that: getting rid of some baggage. It's learning to travel lighter. It is a stepping stone on the path to healing. There is a saying in recovery circles that "we're only as sick as our secrets." While confessing secrets is not itself enough for healing, it is a prerequisite for healing. We really can't begin the process until all the truth is on the table—especially with God.

Unfortunately many men who confess their struggles with sexual sin do so in generalities. This is insufficient. We need to confess details. Even though we know God knows, something significant happens when we confess the details to Him. We grasp the gravity of our sin. We get a little closer to conceptualizing how it grieves His heart. By acknowledging the details of our sin, we take one step closer to releasing each and every piece of baggage. When things are brought into the light, we can be set free.

We see this modeled in the Old Testament sacrificial system. It was intricate and detailed, to cover and atone for specific sins, not just sin in general. Likewise, we should ask God for covering and atonement for specific sins. If you find yourself reluctant to tell God about the details, you may be experiencing denial, which only delays your healing. Denial keeps you stuck; acknowledgment and confession begins to set you free.

While confessing to God is the first and most important step, we must also confess to another person for healing to fully occur. How can anyone pray for you if they don't know what you're struggling with? How can anyone offer any hope or suggestions if they don't know the reality of your situation? They can't. They won't. Also, as with God, we must confess the details to another person. Someone needs to know us and the reality of our behaviors, thoughts, and intentions. We must face the potential rejection and shame of their response. In confessing to another person, we bring accountability into our life, as well as someone who can walk alongside us in encouragement and support.

We can never fully accept acceptance until we're fully known, because we'll always have the little voice in our head saying, "If you really knew me, would you still accept me?" Speaking the truth about your past and your struggles is the only way to find the answer to this question. And with God, the answer will always be yes.

Confess to God and another person. Unload some baggage. It's time to travel lighter.

 SELF

Are there specifics of your story that need to be confessed? Behaviors, thoughts, or even the state of your heart can all be fair game for confession.

What do you feel when you consider confessing to God and others? If there is fear, what are you afraid of?

Think for a minute about being the recipient of others' stories. When people you care about share their lives, especially the shameful parts, does it engender acceptance or rejection towards them? If it's acceptance, can you trust that they will likely give the same acceptance to you?

STOP STEALING

> **Ephesians 4:28**
>
> *Anyone who has been stealing must steal no longer, but must work, doing something useful with their own hands, that they may have something to share with those in need.*

DEVO

Have you ever considered that acting out sexually is actually an act of stealing? It is stealing from ourselves. We rob ourselves of peace, respect, and self-confidence. We rob ourselves of joy and of intimacy in relationships.

It is also stealing from others. It robs others of their dignity and their humanity. Plus, somebody, somewhere on the planet misses out on us when we are acting out. It could be wives, children, friends, or even strangers that God wants us to impact. But we can't—because we're absent, whether mentally, emotionally, or physically.

Finally, it is robbing God. He is robbed of the glory He deserves by our lives reflecting His goodness and character. When we act out sexually, everyone ends up with less than they deserve.

In the verse above, Paul tells us we are to stop stealing and start working—so much so that there is an overage, an abundance. Out of that overage we can give to someone else and, in turn, they can stop stealing too. In the overflow of our lives God is proven sufficient and He is glorified. He longs to use us redemptively for his purposes. He desires to use us to bless others. As we work towards abundance, to be used by God, we will find our focus and energy spent on Kingdom things rather than on selfish things. When our hearts, minds, and hands are set on things above, they cannot be set on the flesh. Figuratively or literally!

👤 SELF

How have you been robbed by your sexual acting out? What, specifically, have you lost or missed out on due to your sin?

Who else have you stolen from and how? It may be symbolically, or even literally. What have others been deprived of due to choices you've made?

 GOD

Repent and acknowledge how sexual acting out has ripped off God. Ask Him to show you how redemption is possible, and what it means to work towards abundance today.

Remember— redemption is possible. We have to seek it, but God's deepest desire is to redeem us and bring wholeness into our lives.

 **OTHERS**

Talk with your connections about how you experience the reality of ripping people off. Have you ever thought about it as such? Ask them for feedback and see if they can identify anywhere else in your life there has been thievery.

Also talk with them about what it means to produce abundance. How can your work benefit someone else? How can they see the possibility of redemption in your life? Write down their responses below.

🙏 GOD

Prayerfully engage confession with God. There need not be any religious formality to it. Simply have a conversation with Him, telling Him what you think needs to be confessed. Then ask for him to bring to mind anything else that should be disclosed, even things you may be hiding from yourself.

OTHERS

You know what's coming next. The things we are most ashamed of are the things we most need to tell someone. Pick a person you trust and get rid of that old baggage.

A QUICK CHECK-IN

Have you been reciting the Romans 8:1 verse? If not, consider this your reminder! (See page 9 for the *Not Condemned* devo).

> **Romans 8:1**
>
> *Therefore, there is now no condemnation for those who are in Christ Jesus.*

Recite Romans 8:1 aloud three times, personalizing the language. (e.g. "Therefore I, (*your name here*), am not condemned, because I, (*your name here*) am in Christ Jesus.")

PATIENCE

> **Romans 5:3-4 (MSG)**
>
> *There's more to come: We continue to shout our praise even when we're hemmed in with troubles, because we know how troubles can develop passionate patience in us, and how that patience in turn forges the tempered steel of virtue, keeping us alert for whatever God will do next.*

DEVO

Waiting is one of the hardest things in life. I highly dislike waiting, especially when I feel like God is up to something. My first inclination is to believe that it will be a long wait, and that maybe what's on the other side won't be worth it. However, I'm starting to believe that maybe its not all about the end, but instead the means to the end. Perhaps a time of waiting is about character development and sanctification rather than an outcome.

Take into account all the potential character development in waiting: control giving way to surrender, pride turning to humility, self-reliance moving toward God-reliance (aka faith), finishing poorly or not at all instead becoming perseverance, doubt transforming into hope. It becomes obvious how waiting is potentially a very effective tool for sanctification.

God wants to mature some of these things in us. There is a reason He hasn't intervened when and how you or I would want Him to. His timing is perfect. He knows when interceding prematurely would hamper our growth. And He knows when we've waited long enough. Perhaps like me, you've prayed a thousand times for God to take your struggle away, and He is silent. This can feel incredibly frustrating, or disheartening, like God has forgotten you. But perhaps His silence is actually His way of saying, "Keep waiting, I'm doing something in you, and I'll be there in due time." Some things take a long time, and can't be rushed. We can't expect powerful, soul-deep transformation to happen overnight either!

Don't lose hope in your waiting. Instead, shift your focus to what character traits could be further developed in your sanctification journey. Look at what God might be trying to cultivate in you.

Remember, He'll be right on time.

 SELF

Do you interpret God's apparent silence as rejection? Or do you believe He is telling you to keep waiting on Him? What character traits have you seen develop in yourself in times of patient waiting?

If you had to choose from the list of character traits listed below, which one would you say needs the most work in you? How do you see immaturity in this area affecting your life?

SURRENDER

HUMILITY

FAITH

PERSEVERANCE

HOPE

🙏 GOD

Do you believe God's timing is perfect? Can you accept that His answer to your prayers may be "Keep waiting"? Does it feel risky to ask Him, yet again, to show up in your life? Prayerfully tell Him your answers to these questions. Ask Him to help you trust in His timing, and to help you be aware of the places where He might be trying to grow you.

 OTHERS

Invite feedback from those closest to you as to what character traits they see developing in you. Ask them to identify what traits need more work and focus. Jot down their feedback below.

AFFLICTION

> **Psalm 119:67**
>
> *Before I was afflicted I went astray, but now I obey your word.*
>
> **Psalm 119:71**
>
> *It was good for me to be afflicted so that I might learn your decrees.*
>
> **Psalm 119:75**
>
> *I know, O Lord, that your laws are righteous, and in faithfulness you have afflicted me.*

DEVO

Could it be that God afflicts us, or perhaps allows us to be afflicted, for our own good? But what good? How could good come from the destruction and hopelessness that plagues so many guys struggling with sexual sin?

I think God wants us to learn for ourselves what value there is in His Word, decrees, and laws. I don't know about you, but I seem to learn more from my mistakes than my successes. When I bump up against something that seems like sandpaper on my soul, it stings. It is abrasive. It's painful.

And I learn where the margins are. Don't you?

We learn how our sin impacts us. We learn how it impacts others. We learn how it grieves the heart of God. Ultimately, without that abrasiveness, we might end up even further off the rails.

God may just love us enough to allow us to put our hand on the hot stove. Perhaps in His sovereignty he knows exactly what we need to turn back to him.

OTHERS

Talk with your connections about how you feel afflicted. Ask for their input on changing your perspective; see if they can help you identify places to learn and grow, rather than be bitter, resentful, or just simply resigned.

👤 SELF

Can you see the potential for your affliction to draw you closer to God? Why or why not?

Are there places in your life, other than sexual sin, where you feel like you are being afflicted?

 **GOD**

It seems only prudent to pray for God to remove the affliction and let us up off the mat. After that, let's pray for God to teach us about His righteousness, His decrees, and His faithfulness.

DIVINE DISRUPTIONS

Mark 1:14-15 (MSG)

After John was arrested, Jesus went to Galilee preaching the Message of God: "Time's up! God's kingdom is here. Change your life and believe the Message."

Matthew 27:51

At that moment the curtain of the temple was torn in two from top to bottom.

DEVO

Kairos is a Greek word meaning a limited, opportune time. It is used primarily to identify when God's time intersects human time. When the curtain of the temple was torn, it was that kind of moment; a collision between Heaven and Earth. *Kairos* moments are those moments when God, in His infinite wisdom, decides to disrupt the flow of our time and use it to glorify Himself. I use the term "disrupt" because that is often how it feels to us. We have plans, commitments, places to go, people to see. Time is money; doesn't He know that?

Time is not money to God. Nor is time ours. It is His. He only lets us borrow it. There are instances where He decides to remind us of this by showing us particular places where He would have us move, interact, engage, or pursue something or someone on His behalf. That means using time as He desires us to, not as we wish to. Unfortunately, when we're tangled up in the barbed wire of our egos and sexually acting out we become numb to those moments. We wear blinders that allow us to see what we want to see, not necessarily what we need to see. We wear earplugs and selectively listen to what we want to hear. That makes us even less aware of the Holy Spirit's movement in our life.

Today we can take off the blinders and intentionally be aware of how God wants to intervene in our lives. Perhaps this Divine Disruption is just what you need to remember that God is real, does care, and wants to be active in your life.

 **SELF**

When was the last time you felt like God was disrupting your life with a request for action? Were you obedient?

Think of a time when you are fairly certain the Holy Spirit was urging you to do or say something and you resisted. Why did you resist?

 GOD

Pray for the blinders and earplugs to be removed. Ask God to intervene and for the Holy Spirit's prompting. Then pray for obedience to follow through on what is asked of you.

When we commit to telling the truth, even when it hurts, we begin to align ourselves with God. It is in His truth that we find our true identity.

 SELF

What truth do you need to tell today? Are there any lies that you need to correct, perhaps in the form of embellishments?

Identify one positive truth about your identity in Christ that you can meditate on today. Hopefully it is handy and readily available because you've got a visual cue! Then, when you feel tempted to believe some of the lies you've told, or to create new ones, repeat this verse to yourself.

TRUTH TELLING

1 Corinthians 4:5b (MSG)

When he comes, he will bring out in the open and place in evidence all kinds of things we never even dreamed of—inner motives and purposes and prayers.

Proverbs 12:22 (MSG)

God can't stomach liars; he loves the company of those who keep their word.

John 14:6

Jesus answered, "I am the way and the truth and the life...."

DEVO

Why is it sometimes so hard to tell the truth? If you're like me, there have been times when lies roll off your tongue naturally—more easily than the truth. Perhaps you've found yourself lying about things that are entirely inconsequential. I used to do that too. I realized there were several reasons I lied. One was to minimize consequences. I didn't want to have to face the music when my sin caused other people pain. Another reason I would lie was to protect myself from the reality of disappointment and rejection. If I minimized a situation and painted it in a better light, I wouldn't have to feel so bad about myself. Finally, I did it to manufacture acceptance and significance. I would lie, in the form of embellishment, to make my stories more likable, interesting, and exciting.

One of the problems with telling lies is that we are the ones who ultimately end up believing them. And in doing so we lose touch with the truth of who we are. We lose our identity and our sense of ourselves. We forfeit our true identity in Christ for the false identity contrived by our lies. If we're not careful, we'll end up lost; ping-ponging through life wondering who we are, often frustrated by a nagging sense that we're not who we could be.

MY PERSONAL MISSION STATEMENT

⚙ TAKE ACTION

Kairos moments can happen right before us, yet we are often unaware they are happening. Maybe you've experienced that small prompting where you accidentally click the wrong email address and think, "Hmm, I wonder how he's doing?" Or maybe you happen across a contact in your phone that you haven't noticed in a while and feel a quiet prompt to call and check in with them? There are times when we can sense that maybe we should say something to a coworker or store clerk and encourage them. But often we don't. This week, try to be conscious of those moments and follow through on whatever the prompting is. Then report back to your connections on how you responded to those moments and what it was like to do so.

OTHERS

Talk about how frequently (or infrequently) you experienced Kairos moments this week, and how you responded to them. Invite feedback on your willingness to be obedient.

Ask others about their willingness to engage Divine Disruptions. How do they respond to them and why?

 **GOD**

Ask God to convict you and bring to mind where there might be lies that need to be corrected. Listen for His response today.

 **OTHERS**

Share how you have lied in the past and talk about why you did so. What were you trying to gain or accomplish? Ask for accountability around truth telling.

GOOD MORNING

Psalm 5:1-3 (MSG)

Listen, GOD! Please, pay attention!
Can you make sense of these ramblings,
my groans and cries?
   King-God, I need your help.
*Every **morning***
   you'll hear me at it again.
*Every **morning***
   I lay out the pieces of my life
   on your altar
   and watch for fire to descend.

Psalm 59:16

*But I will sing of your strength, in the **morning** I will sing of your love; for you are my fortress, my refuge in times of trouble.*

Psalm 88:13

*But I cry to you for help, Lord; in the **morning** my prayer comes before you.*

Psalm 143:8

*Let the **morning** bring me word of your unfailing love, for I have put my trust in you. Show me the way I should go, for to you I entrust my life.*

Mark 1:35

*Very early in the **morning**, while it was still dark, Jesus got up, left the house and went off to a solitary place, where he prayed.*

> **Lamentations 3:22-23 (MSG)**
>
> *God's loyal love couldn't have run out, his merciful love couldn't have dried up. They're created **new every morning**.*

DEVO

There is something special about the morning. David seemed to do business with God in the mornings. Jesus did too. Even while it was still dark. For David and Jesus, no one was beating down their door early in the morning. There were no armies or clans to lead, no people to help nor people to hide from. This makes more sense the older I've gotten; especially now with a wife, three little boys, and a business. While it is yet dark, the world can't touch us. We aren't on the hook to parent, husband, be an employee or a boss, or to answer any emails, texts, or voicemails. There is a space, before the hustle and bustle, demands and commands, where the world is at bay and our soul is momentarily insulated. We have only ourselves to contend with. For some of us that comes with tremendous relief, for others tremendous terror.

For David and Jesus, we know that time was spiritual, but I wonder if it was equally something we wouldn't consider so "spiritual." Like perhaps it offered them a break from feeling like life was wash-rinse-repeat? You ever feel that way? I know I do. Or maybe it was just a few minutes for David and Jesus to pray against blowing up life that day. I mean, think about Jesus, functioning in real time, as a real human. Consider the pressures of leadership, raising people from the dead, Godliness, exorcisms, being a one-man Biblical debate team, and so on. Wouldn't you think there were mornings when Jesus parked it on a rock and said, "God, I got nothin'. I'd like to turn some water into wine and just take a little vacay today. So if you don't show up, nothing is getting done. I need you." It can be much the same for us sometimes.

It seems like David and Jesus both had the same idea: set the day on the right track before the crazy train is in motion and going off the rails seems like the only option. We serve ourselves well to do the same thing. Rather than land at lunchtime feeling behind the eight ball, we can begin with new mercies and a right perspective on the world. We can see people through Jesus' eyes, not our own lustful eyes. While we can't anticipate every inconvenience, we can be prepared to see them as Divine Disruptions. We can also find new energy and encouragement. It's when we are red lining and maxed out that medicating and checking out seem like good options. Yet when we start our day with the Lord, we give ourselves a chance to change the pace.

Maybe tomorrow is a good morning to see the dark before dawn.

 SELF

Is morning time with God a part of your regular routine? If yes, is it a function of discipline or a function of relationship?

When you feel like life is wash-rinse-repeat, what starts to happen to your drive, motivation, excitement, and passion? Can you see a correlation to your sexual temptation?

If you committed to mornings just two days a week, what difference do you imagine it might make?

⚙ TAKE ACTION

Pick two mornings this week to be up early and spend time with God. Don't worry about the amount of time. It can simply be five minutes to read and pray—or the 1x2x3 structure we talked about in "The Devil Made Me Do It." For reading, check out Psalms 16 (I especially like the Message version) and 112 for passages that will start your day off with your mind focused on the right things.

GOD

Pray for God to help you remember to set your alarm, wake up early, and to meet you in that quiet space of the morning. Pray for His mercy, strength, and peace. Pray for the way you should go and the willingness to follow. Pray for a pure heart, mind, eyes, and right perspective on the day. Pray for integrity.

OTHERS

Talk to your wife (if you're married) and guys about committing to a couple mornings per week. Tell them which mornings, and agree to check in with them that day and see how/if you experience your day, yourself, or God any differently.

(RE)COMMITMENT

Psalm 37:5-6

Commit your way to the Lord;
  trust in him and he will do this:
He will make your righteous reward shine like the dawn,
  your vindication like the noonday sun.

Lamentations 3:22-23

Because of the Lord's great love we are not consumed,
  for his compassions never fail.
They are new every morning;
  great is your faithfulness.

DEVO

Jesus' commitment was wholly about honoring God. We see in a simple one-liner the crux of Jesus' life: "But please, not what I want. What do you want?" (Luke 22:42, MSG).

We must commit ourselves to that call each day. We need a renewal of mercy from God, as well as a renewal from within ourselves each morning to line our sights on the target. That target is to get more outside ourselves and more into the lives of other people. The more we serve others, the less time, energy, and desire there will be to serve ourselves. The way of Jesus is less of self, more of others. It is predicated on more of God.

Today your commitment might simply be to think more about Him. Or perhaps to follow through on calling someone He's put on your heart. Or telling your wife you love her and are intent on honoring her with your thoughts. Or praying with your kids tonight. Whatever your commitment is, your day must begin with that alignment, just like we talked about in the last Devo.

Are you committed to the Way today?

 **SELF**

What do you need to recommit to today? Is it a way of thinking? Is it a relationship? Is it integrity? Perhaps it is simply a recommitment to not blow up your life by lunchtime; whatever it is, write it down!

 **GOD**

Recommitment prayers can help center us, much like our personal mission statement. They are meant to invite God into our lives.

A recommitment prayer that I often pray goes like this: "God, I want to honor you today. I want to be a conduit of your grace to the people I interact with. Help me honor you with the way I live today." Write down your recommitment prayer below.

 OTHERS

I urge you to make someone else aware of your recommitment. Call, text, email, something. Let them know that you want to be held accountable for it, and put yourself on the hook to check in regularly on it.

HIGH VISIBILITY

> **Esther 4:12-14**
>
> *When Esther's words were reported to Mordecai, he sent back this answer: "Do not think that because you are in the king's house you alone of all the Jews will escape. For if you remain silent at this time, relief and deliverance for the Jews will arise from another place, but you and your father's family will perish.* **And who knows but that you have come to your royal position for such a time as this?"** *(Emphasis mine.)*

DEVO

Do you know the story of Esther? She was a Jewish exile who married the King of Persia. Through a soap opera-like series of events, the king was convinced to issue a decree that all Jews in his kingdom be killed. Now, at the point where the king issued this decree he did not know that his wife, Esther, was a Jew.

I want you to understand the predicament Esther finds herself in. She's between a rock and a hard place. One option is that she risks her life by admitting to the king that she is a Jew. Then on top of that, she has to make a massive request of the king to spare her people. Her second option is to keep the secret that she is a Jew, which means she has to watch as her family, friends and culture all die. In that moment, the fate of the Jewish people rested on her shoulders. Will she remain invisible, where it is safe and secure? Or will she become highly visible, risking potential death for the cause she's called to? No pressure, right!

Sometimes the right decisions require way more attention than we want. And when it comes to sexual integrity issues, it seems like that attention is going to be negative and of potentially deadly consequence; like Esther's situation. Yet, in reality people we love as well as people we may never meet potentially stand to benefit from our risky decision to get visible.

Perhaps you've landed on your continent, in your country, within your community, perhaps even in your career or church for such a time as this?

👤 SELF

Have you acknowledged that your decisions, especially with respect to the way you use your sexuality, will have a profound impact on those you love, and on people you'll never meet? Does that reality come with gravity or awe? Does it come with fear or trepidation?

In what ways do you fight the possibility that you've been placed here for such a time as this? What might change if you fully embraced it? If you have embraced it, how have you seen the ripple effects of your decisions?

What does it mean to you to become highly visible right now?

 GOD

Pray that God will give you a glimpse of the reverberations of your decisions, and will empower you to make wise ones.

OTHERS

Talk to your connections about what situations in your life currently might qualify as "such a time as this." Also, discuss where they can see that your becoming highly visible might make a difference. Write down their responses.

JUST VISITING

Hebrews 11:13-16 (MSG)

*Each one of these people of faith died not yet having in hand what was promised, but still believing. How did they do it? They saw it way off in the distance, waved their greeting, and accepted the fact that they were transients in this world. People who live this way make it plain that they are looking for their true home. If they were homesick for the old country, they could have gone back any time they wanted. But they were after a far better country than that—***heaven*** *country. You can see why God is so proud of them, and has a City waiting for them.*

John 15:18-19 (MSG)

If you find the godless world is hating you, remember it got its start hating me. If you lived on the world's terms, the world would love you as one of its own. But since I picked you to live on God's terms and no longer on the world's terms, the world is going to hate you.

DEVO

Ever have that strange, gnawing feeling like you just don't belong? Like you are trying to find your people and where you click but keep coming up short? Sometimes it's like being on the outside looking in. Feeling like we "fit in" can be so elusive. That's especially true when we're swimming upstream from our culture. Go against the flow of popular ideas, ideals, and philosophies of life and it can be a lonely place. This is especially true when it comes to our sexuality.

In a world of sexual promiscuity, anything goes. "Experts" will say that sex before marriage is a good litmus test of long term success, that porn enhances the sexual experience, and that an open relationship with multiple partners is more fulfilling and wards off boredom in the relationship. To suggest that there was an original design for our sexuality and that sexual integrity actually means some boundaries on our sexual desires is today labeled conservative, narrow minded, and judgmental. The world hates God's authority over sexuality. And the world might hate us too if we try to live out His design with obedience. The truth is, we just don't belong here.

But that feeling, like we don't belong, it's not simply a function of being counter-cultural. It's a beacon calling us onward to our true home. We are transients. Tourists. Earth is a staycation resort of sorts and our souls know we are yet to arrive at our ultimate destination. We have a city waiting for us on the other side of this life and the Welcome Home signs are out.

We weren't designed to call this place home. We're just visiting.

 SELF

Can you relate to that feeling of disconnect, of not fitting in? If so, when do you typically feel it (e.g.: at work, in your family, at church, in your neighborhood)?

When you feel like you don't fit in, how do you explain it? Do you blame yourself, or use self-condemnation? Do you blame others?

For some people, the feeling of rejection and awkwardness that goes along with not fitting in is a driver for acting out. Have you considered how your own acting out might be connected to this? In what ways do you feel like culture contradicts God's original design for sex and sexuality?

🙏 GOD

Pray for God to strengthen you to continue to swim upstream. Ask Him to remind you, through the Spirit and through Scripture, that you belong. Pray a prayer of gratitude that even before we were born, Jesus paved the way, and we can have confidence knowing we are walking in his footsteps.

OTHERS

Talk to your connections about how you fit in with them. Do they accept you as you are? Do you feel like you have a home with them? Also talk to them about how you collectively run counter to the culture, especially with regards to sexuality.

GIVING

> **Deuteronomy 15:10-11 (MSG)**
>
> *Give freely and spontaneously. Don't have a stingy heart. The way you handle matters like this triggers GOD, your God's blessing in everything you do, all your work and ventures. There are always going to be poor and needy people among you. So I command you: Always be generous, open purse and hands, give to your neighbors in trouble, your poor and hurting neighbors.*

DEVO

In terms of finances, chances are you probably find yourself somewhere between poverty and riches. Granted, if you are in a first world country, you are likely rich by comparison to the rest of the world. For the sake of this conversation, we'll go on the assumption that there are plenty of people around us who are wealthier than we are, and there are plenty of people around us who are more impoverished than we are. Then there are the poor and needy. We see them on street corners, under the overpasses, roaming around gas stations and huddling in many downtown parks. Sometimes, if you're like me, I have compassion and feel for their plight. Other times I am indignant and arrogant, questioning why they aren't getting jobs and working for a living like the rest of us. I often go into a rant in my head about how broken the "system" is that it can't handle these people. I'll dream about a benevolence spree among corporations that would fund housing and rehabilitation programs, mental health treatment, and medication to get these folks off the streets and to become productive members of society.

Then I remember what the Scriptures say—these folks will always be with us. And what am I to do? What are you to do? And what does this have to do with sexual integrity?

The link to sexual integrity is found in the state of our heart. Our unwillingness to give of time and treasure to those in need points to a selfish and self-centered mentality. Moreover, the essence of stinginess or greediness is to believe we are entitled to something and thus have a right to take it. Often, we will indeed take it at others' expense.

Like taking an eyeful of gawking to satisfy our lustful desire, at the expense of someone else's dignity.

Or taking advantage of someone else's body and sexuality at the expense of their self worth, all the while convincing ourselves that its merely a financial transaction to them.

You see, when we jettison the entitlement and arrogance in some areas, the effects ripple into other areas of our life. Perhaps parting with some time and money on behalf of the poor and needy would develop a deeper sense of humility and integrity. In turn, those might influence our sexuality, such that we move farther from acting out again.

SELF

When you see the poor and needy, do you find yourself going down the indignant and judgmental path like I do? Do you find yourself crying "foul and unjust" when you see folks receiving handouts?

Identify how you've been selfish financially, with your time, and with your sexuality. Are there places where you could part with things you often feel entitled to?

 **GOD**

Pray for God to create opportunities to live unselfishly. Ask Him to show you where you might be tangled up in arrogance or entitlement. Ask for the Holy Spirit to change your heart to live unselfishly as it pertains to your sexuality.

Invite God to show you a specific way to take action

 OTHERS

Talk to your accountability partners about what you might do to live unselfishly. What action step can you take? If the action item doesn't elicit any emotion (perhaps some fear) and doesn't provide you an opportunity to learn something, you probably aren't going far enough outside your comfort zone.

Make yourself accountable to follow through on your Take Action item below. Then be proactive to report back on how that time or event went. Talk about what you felt, learned, saw, and heard.

 TAKE ACTION

Commit to a time and place where you can part with money and/or time in an unselfish manner, and help the poor and needy. Perhaps it's volunteering at a soup kitchen on a Saturday morning? Or maybe giving $5 to a homeless man on a street corner? It doesn't have to be a huge commitment or expense, but it should prompt you to an awareness of how you view the gifts God has given you (time, money, security, community), and where you can make space to put those gifts in service of the Lord—since they truly belong to Him in the first place.

HAS MAT

> **Mark 2:11-12**
>
> *"I tell you, get up, take your mat and go home." He got up, took his mat and walked out in full view of them all. This amazed everyone and they praised God, saying, "We have never seen anything like this!"*
>
> **1 Peter 3:15**
>
> *But in your hearts revere Christ as Lord. Always be prepared to give an answer to everyone who asks you to give the reason for the hope that you have. But do this with gentleness and respect...*

DEVO

In the day and age when the above narrative in Mark 2 occurred, people who couldn't walk laid on mats. It comforted them and made the hard ground a little softer. It was known, throughout the culture, that "crippled" people and mats went together. So why would Jesus instruct someone He had healed to take their mat? If he didn't need it anymore, why carry it around?

The answer: the mat functioned as a daily example of Jesus' healing power in their life and a humble reminder of where they came from. So many men I talk to want to forget their past struggle/addiction and don't want to talk about what they still struggle with. They want to leave it all far behind. But I don't think Jesus wants us to forget our past. Not that we need to dwell in the guilt and shame of our old sinful nature, but too easily we can become prideful about our freedom. If you long to forget the struggle with sexual sin, I urge you to change your perspective. Maybe God doesn't want you to leave your mat behind; perhaps He wants you to keep it close by as a reminder of His faithfulness and goodness.

And perhaps there is an even bigger reason: so that you'll have opportunity to speak of Him! When people saw the man Jesus had healed carrying his mat around, it begged questions. "What happened?" "Why ya got that mat?" "You aren't crippled, so what gives here?" God might just have in mind to utilize your mat as a talking point. When someone asks about your changed life, it gives you a chance to acknowledge Him and how He has shown up.

Keep your mat handy. You never know when God might want to use it.

 SELF

Are you hesitant to carry your mat as it pertains to sexual integrity issues? Do you sometimes wish it were all a distant memory? Why or why not?

Can you identify any other "mats" in your life that you currently carry around?

Are you prepared to talk about integrity issues if someone in need brings it up? Why or why not?

🙏 GOD

Ask God what it means for you to carry the mat of sexual integrity. Ask Him to help you remember Him every time you're reminded what you are being healed from.

OTHERS

Talk with your connections about the mats you carry and what that is like for you. What mats do they carry?

MY PERSONAL MISSION STATEMENT

LEGACY

Psalm 78:1-7

My people, hear my teaching;
  listen to the words of my mouth.
I will open my mouth with a parable;
  I will utter hidden things, things from of old—
  things we have heard and known,
  things our ancestors have told us.
We will not hide them from their descendants;
  we will tell the next generation
  the praiseworthy deeds of the Lord,
  his power, and the wonders he has done.
He decreed statutes for Jacob
  and established the law in Israel,
  which he commanded our ancestors
  to teach their children,
  so the next generation would know them,
  even the children yet to be born,
  and they in turn would tell their children.
Then they would put their trust in God
  and would not forget his deeds
but would keep his commands.

Hebrews 12:1-2

Therefore, since we are surrounded by such a great cloud of witnesses, let us throw off everything that hinders and the sin that so easily entangles. And let us run with perseverance the race marked out for us, fixing our eyes on Jesus, the pioneer and perfecter of faith.

DEVO

God is interested in legacy. He was interested in his own legacy, in his son's legacy, and he is interested in your legacy. We see Jesus as the reflection of God; His legacy. He was a visible, tangible portrayal of the Father's love and mercy. His life was devoted to living out the legacy of the Father. He believed the way of the Father should be His way. And He became the Way. His legacy rolls on over generations, in the most widely published book on earth, through the most powerful movement ever known to man.

The early disciples believed in the legacy so much they carried it on. And the way they lived their lives, chronicled in the Scriptures, became worthy of following. Their legacy is carried on even today. They were sold out on God and His purposes; so much that they left behind everything secure to be a part of the movement.

We also are leaving a legacy. Whether intentionally or not, we are setting an example and a tone for the next generation to follow.

What will your legacy be?

Will it be one marked by bad decisions and unfaithfulness, by besetting and addictive sin patterns? Or will it be one characterized by humility, contrition, boldness, and willingness to change? Will you be known by your stubborn resistance or by how you went all in on God and His purposes? God's desire is for you to leave a positive legacy, one that points this generation and the next to come back to Him. He desires that all of us take the baton pass and run our leg of the race with purpose and passion.

SELF

Consider your legacy. What message are you sending with your life, currently?

Take a few minutes to consider whose legacy you are following. A parent? A pastor? A friend? Don't be lulled into the lie that you are blazing your own trail; we all follow someone's footsteps. Perhaps you're not following someone directly, but instead you're creating a legacy based on the opposite of what someone else has done. Ex: "I'll never do what so and so has done," or "I'll make sure I'm not *that* kind of person." Are you following in the footsteps of someone worthy of emulation?

 GOD

Pray for a lasting, positive legacy. Ask God to show you those areas where your life example is worthy of following, then thank Him for it.

Also ask Him to reveal those areas that need a little work, and invite Him to begin changing you.

👥 OTHERS

Talk about your current legacy and ask for feedback. If the people around you had to identify your legacy today, what would they say? (I have to admit, as I consider asking a few key people in my life, this question is scary!)

TAKE ACTION

It's time for a different kind of mission statement. This one is bigger than before; this is a manifesto of sorts. I urge you to consider a statement that defines **the overarching theme of your life.** What is the banner under which your life is lived? When the end comes and people are talking about your impact on the planet, what do you want them to be able to say? What do you want your grandchildren to say of the legacy you handed down to them?

MY LEGACY STATEMENT

CLOSING

Well, how was it? Did you get anything out of the time you spent in this book? If so, what? Take a minute to reflect on it and identify your takeaways. Has anything changed in your perspective of yourself, your relationships, or of God? What about your feelings towards the Scriptures?

You and I both know that things like this are good for a takeaway or two. But they usually don't have profound effects from here on out because we forget what we learned and stopped taking action. I don't want that to happen. I hope you'll continue some of the practices of the various devos. Keep your visual cues up, and update them or move them when they get stale. Continue practicing your recommitment prayer. Utilize the visualizations and replacement thoughts. You get the picture.

Did anything shift in the way you connect with others? Hopefully there were some really uncomfortable conversations over the course of reading this book. And hopefully some really encouraging ones. And some where you had voice to speak into others' lives. Even if you got nothing else out of it, that is entirely worth it to me.

Going forward I'm glad to help you if there is something I can do. Get you connected with help, get other resources to you, whatever that looks like. Feel free to reach out: **Jason@redemptiveliving.com**.

Stay on the journey. You can do it. God will help.

Jason

ABOUT THE AUTHOR

After sexual addiction almost took his life and his marriage, Jason was called to help other men. He has a Finance degree from the University of Oklahoma and began his career in the corporate world as a consultant with Arthur Andersen and Interstate Batteries. The recovery process led him out of corporate and into ministry to obtain a Masters in Counseling from Denver Seminary. Today Jason is the President of Redemptive Living, a ministry devoted to helping men and marriages find redemption after betrayal. He is the National Speaker for the Every Man's Battle Workshops, and regularly speaks at churches, conferences and men's events. He has invested over 10,000 client hours specializing in sexual integrity work. His books include Worthy of Her Trust, Understanding and Loving a Person with Sexual Addiction, and the Summit Devotional. Along with Shelley and their 3 boys, Jason is happy to call Denver home.

 **redemptiveliving**

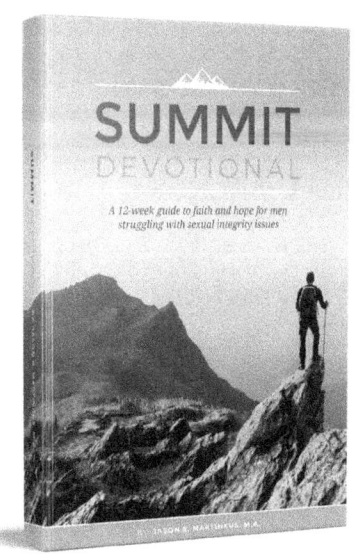

For more information and resources, please visit
WWW.REDEMPTIVELIVING.COM

Kitchen CONVOS

Take the guesswork out of the process and accelerate your healing.

THROUGH OVER 30 VIDEOS & THE INCLUDED WORKBOOK, THE COURSE PROVIDES PRACTICAL GUIDANCE & TOOLS TO WALK YOU THROUGH THE **HEALING PROCESS.**

- Disclosure/ discovery
- The grieving process
- How to handle anger and what role it plays
- Where relapse happens and how to avoid it
- The origins of Shame and how it drives acting out
- The Addictive Cycle and how to pull the ripcord and exit
- The Intimacy Aversion cycle and how we can engage rather than retreat
- How to handle triggers for wives / How to help your wife handle them
- How to rebuild deep, connected intimacy

> KitchenConvos is an absolutely unparalleled resource for couples going through recovery and healing from sexual betrayal or addiction.
>
> – LISA TAYLOR, CERTIFIED PASTORAL SEX ADDICTION SPECIALIST

WWW.KITCHENCONVOS.COM

www.ingramcontent.com/pod-product-compliance
Lightning Source LLC
Chambersburg PA
CBHW060528010526
44110CB00052B/2536